MW00849405

Kingdom Wisdom Devotional

for Graduates

**Books by Tony Evans
from Bethany House Publishers**

Kingdom Men Rising
Kingdom Men Rising Devotional
Kingdom Values
Kingdom Values Devotional
Kingdom Kindness
Kingdom Wisdom Devotional for Graduates

Kingdom Wisdom Devotional
for Graduates

**90 Days of God's Promises
for Young Men**

Tony Evans

BETHANY HOUSE
a division of Baker Publishing Group
Minneapolis, Minnesota

© 2025 by Tony Evans

Published by Bethany House Publishers
Minneapolis, Minnesota
BethanyHouse.com

Bethany House Publishers is a division of
Baker Publishing Group, Grand Rapids, Michigan

Printed in the United States of America

Library of Congress Cataloging-in-Publication Data
Names: Evans, Tony.
Title: Kingdom wisdom devotional for graduates : 90 days of God's promises for
    young men / Tony Evans.
Description: Minneapolis, Minnesota : Bethany House Publishers, a division of
    Baker Publishing Group, [2025] | Includes bibliographical references.
Identifiers: LCCN 2024039021 | ISBN 9780764243516 (cloth) | ISBN 9781493449651
    (ebook)
Subjects: LCSH: Young men—Religious life. | Christianity—Prayers and devotions.
Classification: LCC BV4541.3 .E38 2025 | DDC 248.8/32—dc23/eng/20240925
LC record available at https://lccn.loc.gov/2024039021

Portions of this book were adapted from *Kingdom Men Rising Devotional* (Bethany
House, 2021) and *Kingdom Values Devotional* (Bethany House, 2023) by Tony Evans.

Cover design by David Carlson, Studio Gearbox

Baker Publishing Group publications use paper produced from sustainable forestry
practices and postconsumer waste whenever possible.

25 26 27 28 29 30 31   7 6 5 4 3 2 1

To my grandchildren
Kariss Farris, Jessica Hurst, Jackson Shirer, Jesse Hurst,
Jerry Shirer, Kanaan Hurst, Jude Shirer, Joel Hurst, Kelsey Evans,
Jonathan Evans II, Kylar Evans, Kamden Evans,
and Jade Wynter Evans

And great-grandchildren
Lois Farris, Joshua Farris II, Josephine Farris,
Evelyn Farris, and Selah Farris

Introduction

I remember being a young man, striving for a vision of where I was supposed to go and what I was supposed to do. Asking myself, *What do I want for my life—but even more important, what does God want for me?* This is going to be one of the toughest questions you'll ever face, and no one else can answer it for you. As you go out into the world, you're stepping out from under the authority of others into your own adventure, and you will have to find your own path rather than relying on others to choose your path for you.

The world is a different place than it was when I was a young man. Back then our culture generally accepted a Judeo-Christian worldview. Not so today. Young men have a steeper hill to climb, and it's more important than ever to know the difference between lies and the truth.

So where should you go for answers? There's no better source than the Lord himself. Ask God to give you the vision you seek, and let Him show you what you should be striving to achieve personally, spiritually, and professionally. He is the one authority you will always be under—from now until the end of time. So seek His compass and you'll never be steered in the wrong direction.

The compass He provides is His Word, so ground yourself in the Bible, letting it define what it means to be a man and what your priorities should be. Then look for outside sources to reinforce a biblical worldview—fellowship, books, and a local church that holds closely to Jesus and God's Word. All of these things will help you to distinguish the truth from lies.

Look for others who are headed in the same direction; encourage them and let them encourage you. And at the same time, seek to avoid the traps the world has set for you—dangerous social media, bad relationships, and teachers who are trying to push you away from God and toward the philosophies of today. Like David, you want to be on God's side in every battle, and to do that you've got to know what Goliath looks like.

As you venture out into the world, may God bless you and guide you. Pursue being a man after God's own heart, pleasing heaven while making a difference here on earth.

> Therefore, I urge you, brothers and sisters, in view of God's mercy, to offer your bodies as a living sacrifice, holy and pleasing to God—this is your true and proper worship. Do not conform to the pattern of this world, but be transformed by the renewing of your mind.
>
> Romans 12:1–2 NIV

For it is God who is at work in you, both to will and to work for His good pleasure.

Philippians 2:13

Reflection

You have been created by God with a specific post He wants you to fulfill and a purpose He wants you to live out. He has scouted you, pursued you, and drafted you for His team. You have a divinely orchestrated reason for your manhood. Now, I know the culture wants to give you a whole slew of other reasons for being a man, but God says clearly that He created you for something great.

Granted, that purpose may seem elusive right now. Instead of looking for your purpose, look for God. After all, He knows your purpose. Once you find Him and become intimate with Him, He will reveal it to you.

God has placed your purpose in you in seed form. You grow that seed through an intentional pursuit of Him. When you learn His ways like an athlete learns the plays, desires, and instincts of a coach, you will align yourself with all that is needed to maximize your potential. Your effort involves aligning yourself within His grid and with His design. God will bring about your greatness. You don't need to force it; you don't need to manipulate to get it or obsessively work toward it. Draw close to God, and He will fulfill your purpose—both for you and through you.

Action

1. Describe your approach to pursuing an intimate relationship with God.
2. In what ways can you strengthen this approach?
3. What one thing from your answer to the previous question are you willing to implement this week?

Prayer

Jesus, help me not to get distracted by pursuing my purpose rather than looking to You. You know why I am here and what I am to accomplish. You know what I need to do to experience the greatest fulfillment of my personal destiny. Draw me near to You and enable me to know You more fully and to hear You more clearly every day. In Your name, amen.

DAY

2

A plan in the heart of a man is like deep water,
But a man of understanding draws it out.

Proverbs 20:5

Reflection

An authentic spiritual life doesn't come through rituals, clubs, programs, or even religion. Spiritual life, power, and strength come
from the Spirit. The closer you are to the Spirit, the more abundant
life you experience and the more influence you will have (John
10:10; 15:7). The further you drift from Christ's Spirit, the more
chaos and dysfunction you experience in the various aspects of
your life.

An important part of maturing spiritually comes from healing
in those areas that hold you back. Forgiveness frees you from the
slavery of self-pity and blame, both of which make you ineffective
for the kingdom of God. You must intentionally pursue personal
spiritual growth, maturity, and mental and spiritual health if you
are to have a lasting impact on the lives you touch.

As we all grow and develop individually, we will be better able
to identify, own, and address the issues plaguing us on many
fronts today, relationally, culturally, and otherwise, including issues within the body of Christ. As a young man trying to follow
the Lord, you must own your role in guiding others to the one true

King. It's time we awaken not only ourselves but also those around us so we will take to the field and overcome the enemy's opposition.

Action

1. On a scale of one to ten, how much of the spiritual "abundant life" do you feel you are experiencing?
2. What can you do to move that number higher on the scale?
3. Why is spiritual maturity an ongoing pursuit rather than a one-time goal?

Prayer

Jesus, draw out the plans You have for me from the depths of my understanding and bring them to the forefront of my awareness. Help me to see the swiftest route to spiritual maturity so that I can take it fully without fail. Give me grace to grow and experience all that I am meant to be, for Your glory and others' good. In Your name, amen.

These things I have spoken to you, so that in Me you may have peace. In the world you have tribulation, but take courage; I have overcome the world.

John 16:33

Reflection

A storm in Scripture often does not refer to a literal storm but to an adverse set of circumstances. When the Bible speaks of a storm, the writer may be conveying negative events entering into a life. A storm connotes trouble, tribulation, and trials. Storms seek to knock you over—mentally, emotionally, physically, and spiritually. You are either in a storm, just heading out of a storm, or about to experience a storm. This is because life is full of troubles, as our passage for today reminds us. That's just the way it is. Storms tear through towns as well as lives, and frequently at that. It's going to rain, thunder, and hail. On everyone. Both the righteous and the unrighteous are affected by storms.

Storms don't care how smart, good-looking, or popular you are. Hail is hail, and it will dent any car it hits. Wind is wind, and it will destroy any building its tornadic forces push against. Rain is rain, and when it floods it doesn't ask your permission or level of prominence first.

Storms affect us all. Just as they affected the two men's vision of a brighter tomorrow in the parable found in Matthew 7:24–29. That's why it is more important to focus on your response to life's storms than to seek to avoid them. To know that in Jesus, who has overcome the world (John 16:33), you can have peace, even in the middle of the fiercest storm. A young man must build his life, relationships, future, and more on the solid foundation of God's Word if he is to withstand the storms that blow through life.

Action

1. In what ways do you feel that you are well prepared for life's storms? In what ways do you feel like you are not?
2. When things get tough, what are some strategies for not losing sight of the game plan you had set in place for your life?
3. How can you shift from emotional reactions to spiritual responses during life's difficulties?

Prayer

Jesus, rather than living in denial of the fact that storms happen, I want to be spiritually prepared for when they do. Help me devise a solid game plan to approach life's troubles and tribulations from a position of strength. In Your name, amen.

But realize this, that in the last days, difficult times will come. For men will be lovers of self, lovers of money, boastful, arrogant, revilers, disobedient to parents, ungrateful, unholy, unloving, irreconcilable, malicious gossips, without self-control, brutal, haters of good, treacherous, reckless, conceited, lovers of pleasure rather than lovers of God, holding to a form of godliness, although they have denied its power; Avoid such men as these. For among them are those who enter into households and captivate weak women weighed down with sins, led on by various impulses, always learning and never able to come to the knowledge of the truth.

2 Timothy 3:1–7

Reflection

There's a verse in Judges that says, "In those days there was no king in Israel; everyone did what was right in his own eyes" (21:25). And just like back then, decisions these days are primarily made based on feelings. And while that is dangerous in and of itself, it gets even more dangerous when you realize that feelings change. In fact, they can change on a dime. Not only that, but feelings can vary so much from person to person, depending on who you are and what perspective you have.

Feelings don't determine what's true—they never have and they never will. Yet truth is being redefined, and we are witnessing psychological chaos all around us. People's mental trajectory has gone astray because truth no longer serves as a baseline for the mind. We also see philosophical chaos as individuals and scholars doodle with ideas and theories ad nauseam. Scripture calls this ever learning yet never coming to the knowledge of the truth (2 Timothy 3:7).

In order to base your life on God's Word as the ultimate source of truth, you must pursue the knowing of God and His Word with great sincerity and fervor. You must proclaim His Word as much as possible. And you must seek to model His kingdom values in all you say and do.

Action

1. In what ways does consistent time in God's Word help align your thoughts and actions with truth?
2. How does a removal of God's Word from society impact societal values?
3. This week, identify and commit to one way you can increase your awareness and application of God's Word in your life. Write down what you plan to do.

Prayer

Jesus, I want to know Your Word more than I do. Will you give me an increased desire to spend time in Your Word? Show me how practical it is when I apply it to the everyday decisions of my life. I ask that You open my spiritual eyes so I can discern truth from lies in what I hear all around me, and do this primarily by rooting more of Your Word in my mind, heart, and soul. In Your name, amen.

The hand of the LORD was upon me, and He brought me out by the Spirit of the LORD and set me down in the middle of the valley; and it was full of bones. He caused me to pass among them round about, and behold, there were very many on the surface of the valley; and lo, they were very dry. He said to me, "Son of man, can these bones live?" And I answered, "O Lord GOD, You know."

Ezekiel 37:1–3

Reflection

A valley is a low place. It's that place where you have to look up just to see the bottom. The biblical account of Ezekiel and an army of skeletons can be compared to a valley. The bones in Ezekiel's valley jumbled together like too many things stuffed in a drawer, nothing connected as it should be.

I don't expect you to identify literally with Ezekiel's account, or with dismembered bones. But if you think about the meaning behind the story, you may be able to identify with it. Because many young men live dismembered lives. They don't see hope. Their lives—hopes, dreams, relationships—feel broken. There seems to be no light at the end of the tunnel unless it's the light of an oncoming train.

When questions come up about how to improve themselves or what to do with their lives, many young men respond with a shrug of the shoulders. Far too many Christian men are broken. Ezekiel's own words when he was asked if the skeletons could ever rise up may reflect our own. To paraphrase, "Only God knows" (v. 3). That's a polite way of saying, "I don't think any of us know how to solve this. At all." If you read further, however, Ezekiel's story does bring hope, but only when he learns to look to God, and God alone, for the solution to life's struggles.

Action

1. Identify an area or areas in your life that feel like these dry bones.
2. What would it take for you to hope again that God can restore, revive, and redeem what has been broken or lost?
3. Take a moment to ask God to do that.

Prayer

Jesus, show me the life that can be given to the areas of my life that seem dead, dismembered, broken, or lost. Remind me of Your power. Restore my shaken faith. Let me know that it is okay to hope again and believe again because You are able to do exceedingly beyond what I could ask or even imagine. In Your name, amen.

Then He said to me, "Son of man, these bones are the whole house of Israel; behold, they say, 'Our bones are dried up and our hope has perished. We are completely cut off.'"

Ezekiel 37:11

Reflection

Many young men lack answers on how to address the issues in their lives. What's more, they lack the assurance of faith that what seems broken in themselves can ever be restored. Perhaps it's an addiction to porn or alcohol. Could be trouble in school. Or a difficult relationship. Might be a miserable mentality. Whatever has caused so many young men's Christian strength to lie limp on the ground seems to have sucked away hope for a solution as well. Maybe that describes you.

If it does, I would argue that hope has gone primarily because it's hard to fix a problem when you don't know—or choose to ignore— the cause of it. Hope vanishes when we focus on the symptoms and not on the sins that brought the symptoms about. Whenever you are looking for a cure, you must address the cause. Far too many young men are doing patchwork on symptoms rather than dealing with the systemic root issues that have caused the decay. If we are ever to get our lives right, we have to address the spiritual causes beneath the brokenness. We'll look at some possible causes in the upcoming devotions.

Action

1. What happens when you fail to address the cause of a sickness?
2. Describe how that also applies to spiritual sicknesses such as sin.
3. What is an area in your life where you haven't identified the cause of the troubles you face, and which has kept you from either healing or overcoming?

Prayer

Jesus, I want to address the cause of any trials or chaos in my life, family, church, and community. I don't want to keep trying to make the symptoms go away without looking at how to fix the problem once and for all. Give me the courage to peel back the layers of deception or denial that have prevented me from rooting out the cause of sin and its effect in many areas. In Your name, amen.

But your iniquities have made a separation
between you and your God,
And your sins have hidden His face from you so
that He does not hear.

Isaiah 59:2

Reflection

One reason you might feel like your life is dried up in a valley for
an extended time is because of disobedience to God. Disobedience
creates spiritual distance. And any distance from God will lead to
a disastrous level of spiritual dryness. It can be subtle at first. You
may start off on whatever it is you are doing with good intentions,
but if you turn from God along the way, you begin to rebel. Because
it is subtle, it may not feel like rebellion. It may just feel like you are
drifting away from God and His plan and purpose. But the result
remains: You become spiritually estranged. In doing so, you reduce
or eliminate your fellowship with God and devolve into a life that
is just piles of dry bones.

If that sounds like you in any way—if you are dry spiritually,
emotionally, relationally, or in any other way—it is most likely because you are distant from God. And disobedience always leads
to distance. Now, I know that we all have dry times. A young man
can face a slump here or a setback there. I'm not talking about
that. What I'm saying here is that if you find yourself living in a
dry valley where every single day you wake up to no motivation,

no passion, and no spiritual fervor, it is because you have become distant from God. One thing leads to prolonged distance from God: failing to align under the rule of the King.

Action

1. Examine your spiritual closeness to God and rate it on a scale of one to ten, with ten being very close.
2. How do you think relational distance from God has affected your life?
3. In what ways do you think drawing closer to God could bring improvements in your life?

Prayer

Jesus, forgive me for having pulled back from Your will and Your way over the course of my life. Forgive me for every left turn I have taken. Reveal to me what I need to do to draw nearer to You and light the spark of intimacy between us. In Your name, amen.

Then they will cry out to the Lord,
But He will not answer them.
Instead, He will hide His face from them at that time
Because they have practiced evil deeds.

Micah 3:4

Reflection

One way to become distant from God is through idolatry. Now, I know that you probably are thinking you don't worship idols. You might be imagining worshiping a statue, nature, or something else set up as a false god. But idolatry isn't just bowing down to a carved statue stuck on a pole. No, an idol is anything that usurps God's rightful rule in your life. Idols come in all shapes and sizes. An idol could be sports, video games, technology, entertainment, relationships, or any number of things. Idols can even be found in the church.

Idolatry is not just an out-there concept from a distant land. I say that because idolatry centers on alignment: Whatever you align your thoughts, words, and actions under is what you value most.

Have you ever wondered how we can have all these churches and all these books and all these songs, programs, seminars, huddle groups, Bible studies, radio broadcasts, podcasts, and more, and yet still have all this mess? There are idols everywhere; that's how. Somebody, or something, has been brought into God's realm of rule, and there is no room for two kings in any sovereign land. Anytime you turn to other sources besides God and His Rule to meet your needs, to entertain you, or to solve your problems, you have become an idolater. As a result, your life has been set on a path to symbolically lay dormant in a wasteland of a dismembered destiny.

Action

1. Which things, people, or activities in your life usurp God's rightful rule and influence over you?
2. What negative fallout have you seen from placing such things above God's rule?
3. In what areas would you like to see God have greater influence in your life?

Prayer

Jesus, reveal to me those areas where I have sinned and placed something else, or even someone else, above Your rule in my life. Show me the negative results so I can be fully aware of what I have brought upon myself and can learn from it. Help me to draw closer to You and let go of any idols. In Your name, amen.

DAY

9

Therefore prophesy and say to them, "Thus says the Lord God, 'Behold, I will open your graves and cause you to come up out of your graves, My people; and I will bring you into the land of Israel. Then you will know that I am the Lord, when I have opened your graves and caused you to come up out of your graves, My people.'"

Ezekiel 37:12–13

Reflection

When you have drifted away from God—like the Israelites in Eze-kiel 37—you can find yourself in a situation with no earthly so-lution. Any spiritual disconnection can lead to catastrophe. This happens when you are so far removed from God that you can no longer readily identify the cause of the effect. When you fail to make the connection between the spiritual and the social, you will also fail to seek the solution that can bring real and lasting impact.

A failure to address the spiritual root of the physical mayhem will result in your remaining in a valley of spiritual, emotional, relational, or even vocational dryness, unable to rise at all.

Yet in the midst of any problem, we can find a promise. In the Israelites' situation, God made a promise that He alone would open the graves and cause life to exist where death had once dominated. Last I checked, if you are dead and you come up out of a grave, that's a supernatural arising. Thus, the good news of this promise is that no matter how dry you are or how dry your situation is, those bones can live again. If you are dry spiritually, you can live again. If your studies are dry or your friendships are a wasteland, they can rise and prosper again.

If God can take a field of dry bones and cause it to pulsate with life, how much more can He do for you? The question is never *Can God do it?* The question is always *How badly do you want it?*

Action

1. When have you seen God reverse irreversible situations and produce life where there was only death?
2. Identify an area in your life where you would like to see this happen.
3. Take some time to ask God to intervene and turn things around for you.

Prayer

Jesus, I believe You have the power to raise up that which appears to be over and done with. Reveal this power in my own life and show me what I need to do to cooperate with You in this process of restoration. In Your name, amen.

> So Jesus was saying to those Jews who had believed Him, "If you continue in My word, then you are truly disciples of Mine; and you will know the truth, and the truth will make you free."
>
> John 8:31–32

Reflection

You've probably had your car battery go out at some point. I know I have. Standing there looking at that battery won't do a bit of good. Talking to the battery won't change a thing either. It's only when you take a set of cables to connect your dead battery to someone else's live battery that you get the charge you need to drive. That battery gets recharged through the transference of life from another.

Similarly, the only way young men will experience a personal awakening and rise up to fulfill their destinies is through connecting to God's living Word and Spirit. Both are essential before we can experience the spiritual resurrection God offers. It's through His life transferred to us that we will have a transformative influence on our homes, communities, nation, and even world.

It's truth that sets a man free. Not our version of truth—but the truth itself. We discover the truth through reading, learning, and applying God's Word. Sometimes God has to allow us to reach a point of personal paralysis or collective chaos before we are willing to listen to truth.

Action

1. How satisfied are you with the level of engagement you have in God's Word?
2. What is one simple strategy you can apply this week to increase your engagement?
3. Describe the difference between the truth of God and culture's so-called "my truth."

Prayer

Jesus, help me to know You and the truth of the living Word like I never have before. Show me all that I can do to grow in my understanding of truth and in the wisdom of applying it to my life. Show me how to better serve You in everything I do. In Your name, amen.

But Jesus answered and said to them, "You are mistaken, not understanding the Scriptures nor the power of God."

Matthew 22:29

Reflection

It is God's Word that is to order our lives when we read and apply it. Keep in mind that reading it isn't enough. Memorizing it isn't enough. We must apply the truth of God's Word to our decisions in order to receive the benefits obedience brings.

When you choose to live in alignment with the truth and God's precepts, and when you serve in your family, your school, and your community, everyone feels the effect. It is when kingdom men align with God and His Word that we experience order in our lives and the lives of those around us.

But remember, only the Spirit of God himself can pull anything out of its deadened or hopeless situation. That means your top priority right now ought to be cultivating and growing in your relationship with God's Word and getting to know Him better. As you do, you'll awaken. You'll stand. Nothing, and no one, is too far gone from God's powerful hand. He wants you to know that. In fact, that's why God does the supernatural. He revives and restores so that you will recognize His mighty hand and come to know Him more.

Action

1. Why is it important to consistently remain in a state of learning when it comes to God's Word?

2. Are you satisfied with how much you pursue the knowing and applying of God's Word?

3. What would help you to be more motivated to seek God's Word and apply it?

Prayer

Jesus, help me not to get so caught up in pursuing the busyness of life that I forget to go to Your Word for wisdom, direction, and understanding. As I read Your Word, I also ask that You enlighten my heart and my mind with insight. Show me what I need to apply, especially in those areas where I have gotten off track. In Your name, amen.

Behold, I am laying in Zion a stone, a tested stone,
A costly cornerstone for the foundation, firmly placed.
He who believes in it will not be disturbed.

Isaiah 28:16

Reflection

Everyone knows how important the foundation of a home is. If you wind up with cracks in your walls, it is usually due to a faulty or shifting foundation. Today there are metaphorical cracks all around us. There are cracks in our mental health, our relationships, and sometimes our churches too. Cracks have appeared everywhere around and among us. As a result, we spend a great amount of our time, money, and energy trying to patch up the cracks to make things look better. For a while, they do look better. But before long we discover that, given enough time, the cracks reappear.

This is because the foundation keeps moving. The foundation has not been solidified. Any structure that stands on a weak foundation will have cracks in its walls. Any life built on the same will become rife with its own brokenness as well.

This isn't new information. Take sports, for example. Every athlete knows that to be successful you have to strengthen the core. The core, your foundation, controls your ability for movement. A stronger core allows for greater balance, reach, and overall performance. Similarly, a stronger spiritual foundation enables a successful life. Foundations aren't fancy and foundations aren't pretty, but they had better be solid.

Action

1. What are some effects that a faulty spiritual foundation can produce in a person's life?
2. How are these effects showing up in your life?
3. What happens when a faulty foundation is left to crumble over time?

Prayer

Jesus, it isn't ever easy to repair a foundation that is falling apart, but if it's not done, even more damage will occur. I look to You to find out how to repair the foundation of my life where it is faulty. In Your name, amen.

Therefore everyone who hears these words of Mine and acts on them, may be compared to a wise man who built his house on the rock. And the rain fell, and the floods came, and the winds blew and slammed against that house; and yet it did not fall, for it had been founded on the rock.

Matthew 7:24–25

Reflection

In the parable in Matthew 7:24–29, we read about two very different houses. One house stood against the storm. The other house fell due to the storm. Not only did this house fall, but Jesus emphasized that "great was its fall." It didn't just topple over. No, this house came crashing down, most likely destroying everything and everyone in its proximity.

Same storm. Different results. But why? A look at the lives and choices of these two men gives us insight. After all, common sense will tell you that you can't build a skyscraper on the foundation of a chicken coop. The higher you plan to build, the deeper and wider your foundation must be. Our problem today is that we have too many men aiming high without the necessary spiritual foundation to maintain their dreams. One wrong move and the whole thing tumbles down like a badly balanced Jenga game.

Never forget that you will be the foundation. You will be the foundation for so much that happens around you. It's all riding on you and your choices. God clearly declares that men have the primary responsibility for establishing the foundation for all else around them, and even the culture at large.

Action

1. Describe the difference between an emotional reaction to life's storms and the faith to face the storms.
2. In what ways can reacting emotionally to difficulties put you in a worse position to overcome what you are facing?
3. In what ways do you think our culture instructs men to give emotional reactions to issues rather than responses built on faith?

Prayer

Jesus, enable me to not react emotionally to the difficulties I face. Help me to make it through the storms of life as I stand on the sure foundation of faith in You and Your Word. I trust in You and want that trust to rise up in me as courage. In Your name, amen.

But prove yourselves doers of the word, and not merely hearers who delude themselves.

James 1:22

Reflection

The parable of the two men in Matthew 7:24–29 reflects a lot of us today. Many men are asking questions such as, What does it mean to build a life on a solid foundation? How do I create something lasting? Should I build high or wide? Should I go this direction or that? This school or that one? This job or that one? Work this many hours, or that many? Questions like these pummel men's minds like pellets of hail in a summer storm. The rat race has us all running on a wheel at times. But Jesus gives us the answer to all of this and more when He tells us how we can each choose to live as the wise man or the fool. It's simple:

Therefore everyone who hears these words of Mine and acts on them, may be compared to a wise man.

v. 24

Everyone who hears these words of Mine and does not act on them, will be like a foolish man.

v. 26

For starters, Jesus is assuming one thing. He's assuming you're hearing His words. But hearing is never solely the answer. A running back might hear the play called that requires him to rush behind the quarterback to grab the ball. He might hear it clearly. But if he doesn't do it—if he fails to execute the play—the play is most likely over. It's never in the hearing alone. It's always in the doing that makes a man great. The difference between a strong foundation and a weak one is not merely information. You can have a PhD but still be a fool. The difference lies in whether you know how and are willing to apply the information you heard. That's wisdom.

Action

1. Describe the difference between a hearer of the Word and a doer of the Word.
2. What are some things Satan uses to try to keep men from living as doers of the Word?
3. How can you overcome Satan's strategies to keep you ineffective for God's kingdom?

Prayer

Jesus, I want to be a doer of Your Word. I want to live with wisdom in making my choices. This starts with a greater level of discernment. Please give me wisdom and discernment so I will know the right choices to make. Then give me the courage to make them. In Your name, amen.

Therefore, take up the full armor of God, so that you will be able to resist in the evil day, and having done everything, to stand firm. Stand firm therefore, HAVING GIRDED YOUR LOINS WITH TRUTH, and HAVING PUT ON THE BREASTPLATE OF RIGHTEOUSNESS, and having shod YOUR FEET WITH THE PREPARATION OF THE GOSPEL OF PEACE; in addition to all, taking up the shield of faith with which you will be able to extinguish all the flaming arrows of the evil one. And take THE HELMET OF SALVATION, and the sword of the Spirit, which is the word of God.

Ephesians 6:13–17

Reflection

When God did spectacular things in the Bible, He always required the people He was working through to do something first. He told Moses to hold out his rod. He told Joshua to have the priests step into the water. Jesus told those at the tomb of Lazarus to move the stone. He told the disciples to bring what they could find to eat to feed five thousand. Over and over again, God would tell a person, or a group of people, to do something that would then activate the power of His Word.

The reason a lot of young men are not seeing God move miraculously in their lives is that God is not seeing them move in an act of faith. By the way, attending church does not count as an act of faith. Simply hearing the Word will never produce the supernatural intervention of God in your circumstances. Until He detects obedience to and alignment with what He said, you're pretty much on your own. God's authority to overcome obstacles or move you forward in your dreams is activated by action, not talk.

Living as a godly young man requires you to take action that demonstrates your faith in God. The days of passive Christianity are long gone. It is time to stand up for what you believe in, and you do that through your choices.

Action

1. Identify something God has asked you to do in the past in faith but that you did not do.
2. What was the result of your lack of action?
3. Why do you think God wants to see you demonstrate faith through an action before He will show up on your behalf?

Prayer

Jesus, help me to stay connected to Your power and strength through the armor of God. In this way, I will have all I need to be a kingdom man of actions that demonstrate my faith. I ask for Your miraculous intervention in my life, especially in the difficulties I face. In Your name, amen.

But the Spirit explicitly says that in later times some will fall away from the faith, paying attention to deceitful spirits and doctrines of demons, by means of the hypocrisy of liars seared in their own conscience as with a branding iron, men who forbid marriage and advocate abstaining from foods which God has created to be gratefully shared in by those who believe and know the truth.

1 Timothy 4:1–3

Reflection

While Satan may come at you like a friend promising you pleasure, fame, family, or friends, there is one thing you need to realize from the start: Satan is not on your side. He hates you. He is the opponent. And the reason he hates you so much is because you are made in the image of the One he hates most: God.

Sure, Satan may sweet-talk you and act like your friend sometimes, but his strategy is always to take you out. He has studied your game film. He has dug through the clips to discover what motivates you, triggers you, causes you to act or react in a way that he wants. In studying you—and in studying each of us—the devil and his demons know which strings to pull or which buttons to push.

One way to overcome Satan's strategies is by being aware of them. Another way is through consistent prayer. As you go to God each day, ask Him to keep you from the evil one. In doing so, you are asking God to keep you from the wiles of the devil and his attempts to get you off track. This concept is modeled for us in the Lord's Prayer and should be a daily routine in our lives.

A third way to overcome Satan's schemes is through living an authentic life before the Lord. Being honest with God about your own sins and shortcomings and being raw with God regarding your own heart will give you a closer relationship with Him. Deceitful spirits and demons prey on those who live inauthentic, hypocritical lives. They get them into a position where their conscience no longer works by subtly steering them away from God in small increments, as Satan did to Eve when he questioned, "Has God said?"

Action

1. In what ways do you feel that you are successfully overcoming Satan's schemes in your life?
2. Is there anything you can do to make yourself more aware of Satan's approaches in getting you to live outside of God's character and values?
3. Can one person really make a difference? If yes, can you give an example?

Prayer

Jesus, help me live with open eyes and an open heart to see the deceptive schemes of Satan. Show me how to overcome my own areas of weakness and sin so that I can live a holier and purer life, one fully committed to You. I pray this all in Your name, amen.

Peter said to Him, "Explain the parable to us." Jesus said, "Are you still lacking in understanding also? Do you not understand that everything that goes into the mouth passes into the stomach, and is eliminated? But the things that proceed out of the mouth come from the heart, and those defile the man. For out of the heart come evil thoughts, murders, adulteries, fornications, thefts, false witness, slanders. These are the things which defile the man; but to eat with unwashed hands does not defile the man."

Matthew 15:15–20

Reflection

There are many ways to gauge your virtue, but one of the best is by what you say. Your mouth reveals your heart.

When you go to the doctor, they often ask you to stick out your tongue because they are looking for things that could indicate something wrong deeper inside you. The Bible declares that a person's speech also reveals whether there is something wrong deeper inside him or her. What you say, and how you say it, reflects your heart. James 1:26 says, "If anyone thinks himself to be religious, and yet does not bridle his tongue but deceives his own heart, this man's religion is worthless."

Basically, if you can't control your tongue, your "religion is worthless." I understand that occasionally you and I will make mistakes. But what Paul is referring to is the process and revelation of spiritual maturity. If your normal mode of operation is to belittle, judge, gossip, scorn, mock, lie, or engage in any other verbal vice, then you may want to reconsider where your relationship with Jesus Christ sits.

The things spoken come from the heart, revealing the real you. The kingdom of God ought to reflect God's kingdom virtues. You may want to examine where you are today versus where you were several months or a year ago. Has what you say, how you say it, and why you say it fallen more in line, between the goalposts of truth and love, or are you still speaking from the flesh? This is how you can know whether you are growing in godly character and kingdom virtues.

Action

1. How can you remind yourself to let things slide without a biting reply, for the sake of love and kindness?
2. Identify instances when you speak as if what you say is the be-all and end-all, rather than leaving room for someone possibly knowing more than you do.
3. When do your words reflect a heart of faith or fear, calm or chaos, peace or pride?

Prayer

Jesus, help me to glorify You with what I say. I want my words to reflect a heart of faith, calm, and peace, so please work in me to cultivate these kingdom virtues. I know that what I say reveals my heart, so purify my heart with Your love and kindness. I love You, Jesus, and want my speech to mature to a level that pleases You. In Your name I ask this, amen.

But speaking the truth in love, we are to grow up in all aspects into Him who is the head, even Christ.

Ephesians 4:15

Reflection

Let me define *love* biblically. Love is the decision to compassionately, righteously, and responsibly seek the well-being of another. It is a decision, not only a feeling. It is commanded by God, and a command demands obedience. Love always starts off with a decision. It is a decision to compassionately, righteously, and responsibly do or say something for the betterment of someone else.

This means we are to speak the truth in such a way that the person we are speaking to knows our intention is to seek out what is best for them. We are telling them what we are telling them because we want what will be good for them. Obviously, venting would not fall in that category. Neither would gossip, insults, or insinuations. When you and I communicate, according to God's standards of speech, we must communicate in a way that seeks to help. People should know how much we care for their well-being when we communicate with them.

Now, that doesn't mean that we dumb down the truth, but neither does it mean we are to eradicate any concern for feelings. Love does not tolerate all views. Love is not acquiescing to lies. Christians are to love all people, but we are not called to love all ideas.

God makes a clear difference between the sin and the sinner. God loves the sinner. He does not love the sin. Neither does He conflate the two. For example, a loving parent does not accept their child's wrong behavior, and yet they still love their child. And if they are a good parent, they treat their child with love even when they have to correct them. We are always to make a distinction between the action and the person. We are to love the immoral person. We are not to love immorality. We are to love racists. We are not to love racism. We are to love the angry person. We are not to love anger.

Action

1. Why is it important to speak the truth in love?
2. Describe the different responses someone may have to hearing hard truths spoken in love versus hard truths spoken in judgment or condemnation.
3. What would help you to better express truth in love when you are talking?

Prayer

Jesus, create in me a heart of love so that whatever I say to anyone is coming from a space of love in me. I want my words to matter to others, so I want them to be seasoned with grace, peace, and love. In Your name I pray, amen.

Little children, let us not love with word or with tongue, but in deed and truth. We will know by this that we are of the truth, and will assure our heart before Him.

1 John 3:18–19

Reflection

So many people feel free today to correct, judge, teach, or blame people they may not even know on social media. But truth spoken in a spirit and context of love is most often done in an environment of relationships. In order to have relationships, you need to intentionally set out to connect with others. You need to know people well enough to discern when the truth might be needed in their lives. You can't do that if you are never around anybody. The church has many purposes, but one of them is to provide a context for fellowship among believers.

God has given us a community in which we can all thrive when we come together on the basis of two foundational virtues: truth and love. Merging the sharing of truth with love opens the door to a greater experience of God in your life. And couldn't we all use a bit more of experiencing the greatness of God in our lives? God's presence casts out fear. His presence calms the chaos. God's presence ushers in peace, hope, and joy. God allows you and me to feel more of His love from Him when He sees that we are willing to share His love, and His truth, with others.

But what's more is that when you and I make it our habit to live God's way on the foundation of truth merged with a spirit of love, more of our prayers are answered. As we reflect God more in what we say and how we say it, God is more attuned to our prayers.

Action

1. What are some prayer requests you have given to God that have not been addressed yet?
2. What are some prayers that are possibly being hindered through a lack of love in your own heart combined with your not aligning with God's truth?
3. In what ways can you speak the truth in love to a greater degree?

Prayer

Jesus, it isn't always easy to merge truth with love. Help me do the difficult work of purifying my own heart and motives while leaning more deeply into love, empathy, and kindness. Soften my heart to feel a greater level of compassion toward those around me. In Your name I pray, amen.

Now when Jesus saw the crowds, he went up on a mountainside and sat down. His disciples came to him, and He began to teach them.

Matthew 5:1–2 NIV

Reflection

Living a lifestyle that values what God values brings blessings and favor. When Jesus gave what is now called the Sermon on the Mount, He did so because He wanted each of us to know the upside of His values. He also wanted to emphasize that choosing to embrace kingdom values isn't something you do just so you can check off a list. It isn't something you do so you can post virtue-signaling statements online. Neither is it about the need to "grin and bear it" as you seek to live the Christian life. Rather, Jesus paired up each of the kingdom values with a blessing that will boomerang right back to you.

Instead of living a life of chaos, you'll discover calm. Instead of wandering aimlessly in pain, you will find comfort. Instead of going through life unsatisfied, you will find what you need when you need it most. In these eight statements on kingdom values that Jesus made in His Sermon on the Mount, He also provided the purpose behind living them out.

I imagine Jesus gave us the purpose because He knows we are human, needing tangible motivation to spur us on. So He gives us an incentive. He reminds us that when we choose to live and be shaped according to kingdom values, we will be accessing the blessings of God's kingdom for ourselves.

We could all use a bit more blessing in our lives. That's why Jesus urged us to live as His disciples, modeling a life of kingdom values in all we say and do.

Action

1. Describe the difference between a blessing from God and a human reward.
2. In what ways can focusing on human rewards and accolades actually remove the experience of blessings in your life?
3. What do you think is the main reason it is easier to focus on human rewards and accolades rather than to pursue God's blessings?

Prayer

Jesus, help me mold my mind to distinguish between human rewards and divine blessings so that I will know what I am to pursue. I want to walk in the goodness and favor of God's blessings, so enable me to align my heart, mind, and actions under You as the Lord of my life. In Your name I pray, amen.

Blessed are those who have been persecuted for the sake of righteousness, for theirs is the kingdom of heaven.

Matthew 5:10

Reflection

Many people have different ideas about what it means to be blessed. Let's define the term *blessing* from a biblical standpoint. A blessing is a state of well-being in which followers of Christ both enjoy and extend the goodness of God in their lives. It's not a moment of happiness here, nor is it a burst of energy or enthusiasm there. It refers to your ongoing modus operandi. It's a way of life, not an event.

This state of well-being, divine favor, and spiritual stability, also known as *joy* in Scripture, is referred to in the Bible as an inner river that keeps flowing even in times of drought. The work of the Holy Spirit is to produce this in a believer's life. Part of our role in cooperating with our own growth and maturity is to choose to live by the kingdom values outlined for us in the Word of God. When you and I abide in Christ, and thus abide in His Spirit, it is the role of the Spirit to fill us with this inner river—this water overflowing with joy.

The Greek word used for *blessed* in the Sermon on the Mount is the word *makarios*. This referred to Makarios Island, which was off the coast of Greece. It was known at that time as the "blessed island." The natural resources of this blessed island were so rich, fruitful, productive, and thick that those who lived there had all they needed to enjoy their lives to the fullest. They were self-sustained and self-contained and didn't have to go and search for anything else.

Within the biblical concept of being blessed, you will discover all you need to live a fulfilled and satisfied life. As a follower of Jesus Christ, you already have access to your blessing within. You are already on the island called "blessed." You just need to open your spiritual eyes and discover what God has for you.

Action

1. Describe the cause-and-effect relationship between obedience and spiritual blessing.
2. Why do you think God provided an incentive for obedience?
3. On a scale of one to ten (with ten being most blessed), where would you rate your life with regard to receiving spiritual blessings? What could you do to move that number closer to 10?

Prayer

Jesus, I want to live with an open flow from heaven of Your blessings and favor. Show me how to honor You more with an obedient lifestyle and open my eyes to greater opportunities for serving You. In Your name I pray, amen.

And Jesus came up and spoke to them, saying, "All authority has been given to Me in heaven and on earth."

Matthew 28:18

Reflection

Jesus is *the* way to living a blessed life. He knows the way we should go in order to experience the blessings of His kingdom. Just as He spoke to His disciples on the mountainside overlooking the expansive Sea of Galilee, He speaks to us today through His message.

Not too long ago, I was able to visit Israel with my family and ministry partners. One of the highlights of the trip was going up on the mountain where Jesus sat down to teach His disciples and the mass of people gathered to hear. As I stood on the mountainside alongside a film crew and my family, I took a moment to look out over the terrain and imagine what it might have looked like with everyone gathered there. In Matthew 5:1, we read that Jesus sat down to teach. He sat down when He taught on the hillside.

It could have been that Jesus sat down because He was tired. Or it could also have been symbolic. To sit and teach in those days, as it is in our day to a large extent, was to do so from a seat of authority. Like a king sitting on his throne to rule over his kingdom, or a judge presiding over a case, it means to speak from authority.

No one has more authority than Jesus does to deliver the kingdom principles by which we are to live. He is the King of kings. He owns and rules the world we call our home. And since He does, He knows how we are to live in it as kingdom disciples. It's important to rest in the knowledge of His authority because that awareness can give you confidence. But also keep in mind that Jesus wants to improve our lives today because He loves us. It is only when we begin to understand Jesus' heart of love for us that we find His commandments and guidance freeing in our lives rather than constricting. Living with kingdom values is the surest way to live a life of joy, peace, and abundance—which is exactly what Jesus longs for you to experience (John 10:10).

Action

1. How does Jesus' love for you show up in your life?
2. Do you find you respond more favorably and intentionally, or less favorably, when interfacing with someone in authority unbacked by love? Explain why you answered the way you did.
3. How can you shift from robotic obedience, such as simply checking off items on a list, to obeying Jesus out of love for Him?

Prayer

Jesus, I want to know and experience Your love for me the way You shared Your love with Your disciples. Help me come to know Your love on a deeper level than ever before. In Your name I pray, amen.

Blessed are the poor in spirit, for theirs is the kingdom of heaven.

Matthew 5:3

Reflection

Verse 3 of the Sermon on the Mount is a short statement, but it contains a world of truth. "Blessed are the poor in spirit, for theirs is the kingdom of heaven" (Matthew 5:3). Jesus begins by telling us we are blessed when we are poor. Now, I know that nobody in their right mind likes being poor.

Many of us grew up poor. I did. I'm sure many of you reading this book did as well. We grew up without much at all. Some of us grew up eating mayonnaise sandwiches. Some of us also grew up with government-issued cheese or beans, or government-issued powdered milk.

But that's not the poverty Jesus spoke about. Jesus spoke of a spiritual poverty. What's more, He spoke of it in a way that declared this spiritual poverty to be absolutely essential. Spiritual poverty is about humility before God. It's understanding where you are in relationship to Him—that He is the God of the universe, and you belong to Him.

He wasn't condemning money. He wasn't condemning the acquisition of land, animals, or even stuff for a home. In fact, many of God's choicest servants in Scripture were wealthy by today's standards. God had no problem with giving His people financial prosperity in the Bible.

But what He does have a problem with, as indicated by Jesus' opening statement, is when we use our stuff—or our wealth—to measure our spiritual status. For someone to think that God must be closer to them or love them more than the next person just because they have a nice car is to be deceived and void of the true values of the kingdom. Material success does not equate to spiritual success. Sometimes the two can coincide, but that is not always the case and should never be assumed.

Jesus reminded His disciples and those listening that to be blessed in God's kingdom means to intentionally embrace a lifestyle that is poor in spirit.

Action

1. Describe the difference between material success and spiritual success.
2. What are some things Satan uses to try to trick us into believing that material success is the same as spiritual success, if not even better?
3. How can you overcome Satan's strategies to keep you from embracing a heart that is poor in spirit?

Prayer

Jesus, I want to embrace a heart and attitude that is poor in spirit. I do not want to live with puffed-up pride and offend You and Your holiness. In Your name I pray, amen.

For thus says the high and exalted One
Who lives forever, whose name is Holy,
"I dwell on a high and holy place,
And also with the contrite and lowly of spirit
In order to revive the spirit of the lowly
And to revive the heart of the contrite."

Isaiah 57:15

Reflection

To be poor in spirit is to declare spiritual bankruptcy. Being poor in spirit comes through recognizing our total insufficiency to satisfy what is needed in our own humanity to prosper spiritually. When we recognize that our spiritual strength, sufficiency, and abilities are rooted and grounded in Him—because we are poor in spirit— then we will be able to overcome the myriad of things that seem to be coming at us.

Whether it's depression coming at you, or a feeling of defeat, isolation, or grief, or just an overall sense of aimlessness—whatever it is cannot be overcome by you. It is overcome through Christ in you when you recognize His all-sufficiency as King and Lord of all. The world may tell you there's no hope. It may tell you that you will be depressed or a failure for the rest of your life. It may tell you that there is no future for you. But what you must remember, if you are poor in spirit, is that the world doesn't have the last word.

God does. And whatever Satan is using to seek to overcome you, God can overcome when you look to Him to do it.

Knowing this is true, you should always remember that when God puts you in a situation you cannot fix—no matter how much money you have, or intelligence you have, or power you possess—He is doing you a favor. He is showing you your insufficiency so that you can see the kingdom of heaven at work on your behalf. Because once we know enough to declare spiritual bankruptcy, He opens His storehouses of provision to meet us where we need Him most.

Action

1. What would you hope is the outcome of living a life that is truly poor in spirit?
2. Describe why you believe God would want His followers to live with a heart that is poor in spirit.

Prayer

Jesus, help me have a heart that honors You by being poor in spirit. Show me my own self-sufficiency so that I can be convicted by what I see and recognize how useless it is to count on myself when I have You to depend on. In Your name I pray, amen.

DAY

25

For the sorrow that is according to the will of God produces a repentance without regret, leading to salvation, but the sorrow of the world produces death.

2 Corinthians 7:10

Reflection

We read in the Sermon on the Mount that Jesus said, "Blessed are those who mourn, for they shall be comforted" (Matthew 5:4). If we were to change this statement into terms we often use today, it might say, "Blessed are those who are sad or despondent, for they will be comforted." In whatever ways we change the terms, though, most people hearing it would still be confused as to how *blessed* and *mourning*, *sadness*, or even *despondency* can show up together in the same sentence.

After all, we live in a fun, entertainment-based culture. Enjoyment has become one of our premier idols. Most of us want to plow right through any grief or sadness that we experience. In our society, laughter is what is loved. Excitement is what is emphasized. And too often, the desired remedy for any form of sorrow is to medicate it right away.

And yet, Jesus says we are blessed if we cry. We are comforted when we grieve. We gain spiritually when we mourn. None of us can live a life free of pain or disappointment. But sometimes this is exactly what we need to reach a deeper joy on the other side.

Action

1. What are some things you are mourning in your present situation?
2. What have some of the outcomes been from this experience of mourning?
3. Describe any benefits that mourning can bring to a believer's life.

Prayer

Jesus, it's easy to seek fun and entertainment because these things often distract us from emotions we may not want to feel. I praise You and thank You for the opportunities I have to mourn because I know these opportunities can bring me closer to You and Your will for my life—and to repentance—if I respond to them spiritually. In Your name, amen.

Blessed are those who mourn, for they shall be comforted.

Matthew 5:4

Reflection

An important thing we need to understand about God is that one of His chief attributes and characteristics is holiness. He is distinctly holy. Holiness is the state of being "set apart." God exists separate from sin. Sin, to God, is similar to what rotten garbage is to us. No one would want to be in an environment of rotten, smelly garbage—much less to stay there. It isn't a good experience. Because living with the stench of trash, as well as what rotten garbage attracts—rats, ants, flies, and more—would prove to be unsanitary and a health hazard. It's unacceptable.

That's why we take our garbage out, where it gets picked up and delivered to a garbage collection location and dealt with. None of us takes any delight in hanging out with garbage, whether it's our own or someone else's.

But when sin is operating in the life of a believer, he or she is asking a holy God to hang out with garbage. They are saying that even though they know Christ lives in them in the presence of the Holy Spirit, they aren't going to address or remove the filth of sin in their lives. Basically, they are telling God to get used to the smell.

When Jesus gave us the kingdom value of mourning, He was telling us that we were blessed when we have inner anguish over the garbage we've allowed in our lives. We are blessed when we mourn the garbage allowed in the world. We are blessed when we experience sadness for the sinful garbage present in the lives of those we love and fellow believers in Christ. Blessed is the one who is not comfortable with their own or this world's contaminated garbage.

Action

1. What garbage needs to be taken out of your life?
2. Have you ever taken out garbage in your spiritual life and experienced God's blessing as a result? If yes, describe what you learned from that.
3. In what ways does the culture seek to make people comfortable with hoarding their garbage and spiritual sins?

Prayer

Jesus, I do not want to live a life of sin. I want to be clean from sin's contaminants in my life. I confess my sin to You and pray that You will forgive me of my sin and ungodliness. Cleanse me so that I will be clean and holy before God. In Your name I pray, amen.

For the wrath of God is revealed from heaven against all ungodliness and unrighteousness of men who suppress the truth in unrighteousness, because that which is known about God is evident within them; for God made it evident to them. For since the creation of the world His invisible attributes, His eternal power and divine nature, have been clearly seen, being understood through what has been made, so that they are without excuse.

Romans 1:18–20

Reflection

Everybody claims that they want truth in some form or fashion. But when truth comes to the surface, most people can't handle it. That's why a call for truth becomes little more than a call for consensus these days. It is a call for what the culture or the ruling influencers will deem is true—until it changes directions, and another call for consensus goes out.

The problem is truth isn't created by consensus and, what's more, its removal comes with consequences. If and when a culture chooses to suppress truth, that culture will face the consequences of its own choices. This is because you can't be both "poor in spirit" (Matthew 5:3) and think you are the author of what is true. Any time we sidestep and marginalize God's truth, we have leaned into pride. God opposes all forms of pride, and He meets it with His wrath.

In Romans 1:18–20 we read that God unleashes His wrath "because that which is known about God is evident within them; for

God made it evident to them" (v. 19). To put it like a parent would, we should know better than that. God has made truth evident to us.

Everyone is born with a conscience. We have been given a truth-regulator, a smoke detector of the soul. Our conscience knows the truth. Similarly, our conscience knows the smoke and mirrors of a lie. That's why you have probably found yourself innately knowing when something or someone is wrong, or off, or shady. You know this because you are built with a conscience tied to truth.

But the suppression of truth, in time, warps the conscience. Like batteries wearing out in the smoke detector, the conscience becomes less and less responsive or alert. Before you know it, a person's conscience can be buried so deep under a pile of lies that it is difficult for them to distinguish between truth and fiction, right and wrong.

Action

1. What is your personal definition of pride?
2. Why do you think God opposes pride?
3. What do you think God's definition of truth is?

Prayer

Jesus, help me to walk in Your truth and not give in to the pride that wells up within me, seeking to compete with You. I humble myself before You. In Your name, amen.

Blessed are the gentle, for they shall inherit the earth.

Matthew 5:5

Reflection

Many people have a wrong idea of what gentleness means. It does not mean making yourself a pushover. Neither does it mean to become a wallflower. Instead, gentleness involves strength. It involves the wisdom of how to use your strength strategically. Gentleness is actually strength that is directed for a good use while under control. For example, when you are watering your plants in your backyard, it's the difference between blasting water with the spout wide open or diffusing the water into a showering spray.

When Jesus urged His followers to live a meek and gentle life, saying that doing so would bring about blessings (Matthew 5:5), He said this at a time when the Jews were under Roman domination. They wanted freedom from the stranglehold of Roman rule, and because of that, they were looking for a leader who would set them free. Thus, Jesus offered them an effective strategy contrary to what they could think up on their own.

When you use gentleness, you no longer have to try to force things to go as you hoped or planned. You can yield the outcomes to God, who is far stronger and more capable than you, and allow Him the freedom to work things out. Far too many of us actually get in the way of God's showing up and working things out in our lives because we lack this virtue of self-control. We feel like we have to figure things out. We have to solve things. We have to muscle our way through. We have to make our voices heard.

One of the most exciting things in life is to watch God work stuff out for you when you didn't have any idea how it could possibly work out at all. That experience belongs to the meek. It belongs to the gentle. It belongs to those who humble themselves under God and align their lives under His rule. It is reserved for those who are committed to Christ and the will of God.

Action

1. What does the word *gentleness* mean to you?
2. Describe how you feel about living your life in a spirit of ongoing gentleness.
3. Is there a part of you that feels afraid to live with a spirit of ongoing gentleness? If so, describe those emotions and try to identify why they might be there.

Prayer

Jesus, show me how to find the courage to live with gentleness rather than seeking to solve my own problems through my own strength unleashed. I pray this in Your name, amen.

Seek the LORD,
All you humble of the earth
Who have carried out His ordinances;
Seek righteousness, seek humility.
Perhaps you will be hidden
In the day of the LORD's anger.

Zephaniah 2:3

Reflection

If you visit a dentist, my guess is that you would want your dentist to be gentle. In fact, dentists know this and will often include the word *gentle* in the name of their practice to express to patients that this is a high value for them.

Now, if you visit a dentist, you also don't want a dentist who is weak. You don't want a fearful or hesitant dentist. Of course, you want a dentist with confidence, courage, and inner strength. This is a perfect example of what gentleness is. It is not the removal of confidence, courage, or inner strength. Rather, it is the focusing of those traits into a strategic delivery format that is most easily received by those nearby.

You can identify someone who lacks certain basic character qualities, especially meekness, because they lose control. They become angry quickly. They mouth off easily. They get irritated at other drivers or other people posting on social media, or even throw things at the TV. The chaos they put out simply reflects the chaos within.

Gentleness, which comes from having a humble heart, is such an important value to live by that Proverbs 25:28 compares a lack of it to a city about to be overrun by its enemy: "Like a city that is broken into and without walls is a man who has no control over his spirit."

Regardless of strength, skill, power, education, financial wealth, or anything else, it is humility that identifies a person in God's eyes as great. God opposes pride in people because pride dismisses God's hand at work and His rule over all. This kingdom value known as gentleness is a precursor to a heart of gratitude. When you have both, you will be positioning yourself to become truly great in the kingdom of God.

Action

1. Describe the difference between unleashed strength and focused or targeted strength.
2. In what areas do you feel you could improve when it comes to being gentler?

Prayer

Jesus, to be gentle is not to remove my strength from practice, but rather to target it and control it. Help me understand that truth internally so that I will apply this kingdom value more in my life. Thank You. In Your name I pray, amen.

In that they show the work of the Law written in their hearts, their conscience bearing witness and their thoughts alternately accusing or else defending them.

Romans 2:15

Reflection

We all have equal access to a conscience that helps us know the truth. Our conscience has been given to us to bear witness to what we do and say. It is our conscience that guides us in truth and helps us identify deceptive strategies of Satan.

In fact, your conscience ought to make you feel guilty when you think or do something contrary to the truth. It also ought to make you feel confirmed when you think or do something that aligns with the truth.

If you have ever continued in a practice of sin, you'll know the cycle your conscience goes through. You will start off feeling guilty over the sin. But as you continue to move ahead with whatever sinful thought or action you are taking part in, you are suppressing the truth in your own life. You are holding down the manifestation of the truth. You might begin by making excuses. You dismiss any thoughts that you should stop. Eventually, your conscience gets so used to what you are doing that you don't need excuses or dismissals anymore. In fact, your conscience becomes so dulled that it no longer even alerts you to the deception you've adopted as truth.

Your conscience is a gift from God to serve as a regulator for your human heart. While believers also have the Holy Spirit, the conscience is a gift that has been given to everyone. That's why even if a person doesn't have a Bible or doesn't attend church—even if they are not a Christian—there are certain behaviors and thoughts that don't make sense or sit well with their conscience.

Our conscience is a gift that enables us to know God's rules within us. Paying attention to that internal voice known as your conscience will help you live a life that is pleasing to God and beneficial not only to yourself but also to others.

Action

1. Identify a time when your conscience convicted you of sin but you persisted in the thoughts or behavior.
2. In what ways do the media or entertainment try to eliminate the collective conscience toward sin?
3. In what areas of your life have you dulled your conscience? How will you address that?

Prayer

Jesus, forgive me for those areas in my life where I have allowed my conscience to become dull as I continue in sinful thoughts or behaviors. I want to please You and honor You with my life choices, so please give me a greater awareness of the areas in my life where I am living contrary to Your kingdom values. In Your name I pray, amen.

Therefore, putting aside all filthiness and all that remains of wickedness, in humility receive the word implanted, which is able to save your souls.

James 1:21

Reflection

One of the greatest challenges I have when it comes to counseling people as their pastor is the overwhelming number who seem unwilling to submit to God's spiritual authority. They may not want to give up premarital sex. Or getting drunk. Or pornography. I can explain the biblical principles on whatever area they are facing, but if they are not willing to apply those spiritual principles personally, there is no impact. Once a person chooses to live with a rebellious spirit, that person has also chosen to cancel the work of God in their life.

Now, the term *rebellious spirit* may seem strong to you. Perhaps you don't consider making decisions outside of the rule of God as rebellion. Maybe you view it as independence or even personal wisdom. But whenever someone chooses their own way over God's way, it is rebellion against God. It is living with the idea or concept that you know better than the God who made you and who also made the universe in which you live. The only thing that could lead to thinking that way is personal pride. Personal wisdom is personal pride if it does not align under God's overarching rule.

When you bow before God in humility, you will discover your greatest spiritual leverage and strength. You will be able to spot the opponent's tactics more easily than ever before. You will be able to tackle the enemy in the power and might of Christ. This is God's revealed will for you. You are to live as someone who overwhelmingly conquers in Jesus' name. But you only do this through a heart that is willing to go low through surrender and humility before God.

Action

1. Describe the difference between godly wisdom and personal wisdom rooted in your own thoughts.
2. Where have you seen rebellion in your own life?

Prayer

Jesus, my relationship to You rests in humility. You are my Savior, and You rule over all. Forgive me for living in rebellion against You in those times when I have done just that. Help me to honor You with a heart of humility. In Your name, amen.

You invalidated the word of God for the sake of your tradition. You hypocrites, rightly did Isaiah prophesy of you:

> "THIS PEOPLE HONORS ME WITH THEIR LIPS,
> BUT THEIR HEART IS FAR AWAY FROM ME.
> BUT IN VAIN DO THEY WORSHIP ME,
> TEACHING AS DOCTRINES THE PRECEPTS OF MEN."

Matthew 15:6–9

Reflection

Wisdom is both the ability and the responsibility of applying God's truth to life's choices. You can only identify a wise man or a fool by his decisions. Not by the songs he sings in church. Not by the Scriptures he quotes. Many men can speak fluent Christianese. But that all means absolutely nothing unless you are seeking outcomes through aligning life's scenarios with spiritual truths.

Biblical wisdom is about as practical as you can get. It's always tied to the day-in, day-out decisions based on what a person thinks, says, and does. When you choose God by your actions, you activate the divine programming from the Word to go to work for you in bringing about good results.

Do you know what happens if you mix rock with sand? You get sandy rock. It's not solid. When you do this spiritually, it's what we know as *human wisdom*. It's man's point of view with a little Jesus sprinkled on top. But any time you apply human wisdom to life's issues, you get the same disastrous result as you would if you added a bit of arsenic to your stew. When you do this, Matthew 15:6 says you have canceled out the power of God's Word. When you bring man's point of view and it contradicts God's point of view, in attaching that to God, you attempt to override God's truth. Thus, you also shut out His strength and divine intervention in your life.

Action

1. What are some ways our Christian culture has added human wisdom to God's truth?
2. What are some of the results of this mix?
3. Read Matthew 15:1–9, then describe Matthew 15:6 in your own contemporary understanding.

Prayer

Jesus, it's easy to get caught up in mixing human thoughts into Your Word and then calling it "my truth." The problem is "my truth" isn't the truth and isn't going to be there for me when I need it to be. I need You to set me free from life's troubles with the truth that has all power. I ask for this in my life. In Your name, amen.

"For My thoughts are not your thoughts,
Nor are your ways My ways," declares the LORD.
"For as the heavens are higher than the earth,
So are My ways higher than your ways
And My thoughts than your thoughts."

Isaiah 55:8–9

Reflection

Far too many people treat the Bible like they do the monarchy of England. They'll give the institution some props. But they will not give it any power because it does not have the final say. Similarly, until you and I develop a radical understanding of Scripture's authority in our lives, it will be of little use to us.

Scripture is the revelation of God. It is God's primary way of disclosing to us all He wants us to know. Scripture reveals to us the whole story. It is God giving you and me the content He wants us to have to guide us, lead us, and show us the best ways forward. As He says in Isaiah 55:11, His Word has a purpose. His Word will accomplish what He desires because His Word has the authoritative power of truth.

We need to pay attention to Him and His Word more than anything else because God reveals His heart and His thoughts in His Word. We can't guess what God is thinking or assume we know what He is thinking because He doesn't think like we do. His thoughts are not our thoughts. He doesn't roll like us. His ways are not our ways. In fact, they are not even close to our ways. As high as the heaven stretches above the earth is how different we are from God. We are finite. We think of things from a limited perspective. God is infinite. He knows all.

Any time you or I try to figure something out independently of God, we start down the pathway of confusion. God operates and functions on a whole other level. When we align our thoughts with Him, we discover the peaceful gift of clarity. This is because the words that proceed out of God's mouth are not empty speech. He speaks purposefully. God is always intentional.

Action

1. What happens when you fail to study God's Word and meditate on it?
2. When have you assumed you knew what God was thinking, only to discover His plan went beyond your scope of thought?
3. How can you apply to a situation you are struggling with today what you have learned in regard to assumptions about God's thinking?

Prayer

Father, Your thoughts are beyond me at such a high level that I shouldn't even try to presume that I know Your plans. Guide me into Your plan and purpose for my life as I draw closer to You in a heart of worship and trust. I pray all of this in Jesus' name, amen.

Blessed are those who hunger and thirst for righteousness, for they shall be satisfied.

Matthew 5:6

Reflection

Appetite is one of the great indicators to a doctor of your health. Consistent loss of appetite is an indication of a much deeper problem. That's why one of the first questions a nurse or a doctor will ask when you go in for a visit is how your appetite has been. Similarly, spiritual appetite is one of the great indicators to God of your spiritual health. If you experience no appetite for Him and His truth or values, then you are revealing a lack of felt need for and connection to Him.

While we all have experienced hunger from time to time, it's true that we live in a day when most of us don't have to worry about being hungry for very long. Access to food in the Western world is abundant. It wasn't like that in biblical days, though, when there were no freezers or refrigerators. People had to hustle after food day in and day out because it couldn't typically be preserved for extended periods. In addition, food preparation was often laborious and a lengthy process.

Many who lived in the day and age in which Jesus spoke of hunger and thirst knew exactly what it was like to feel hungry. They knew what it was to be thirsty. They knew what it was like to have gone an extended time without the nourishment they needed.

Real hunger can be so deep and so gnawing that it can literally hurt, keeping a person awake all night. This is the hunger and the thirst Jesus spoke about. This is how we are to feel toward obtaining righteousness in our lives.

Action

1. Describe a moment in your life when you were so hungry that it affected what you could do or think about.
2. What did you choose to do about it?
3. What can this experience teach you about the level of hunger you are to have for righteousness?

Prayer

Jesus, You have taught us that we are to hunger and thirst for righteousness, so I want to do this in a way that pleases You. Help me gain a better understanding of what this means and what this looks like in my life. In Your name I pray, amen.

Why do you spend money for what is not bread,
And your wages for what does not satisfy?
Listen carefully to Me, and eat what is good,
And delight yourself in abundance.

Isaiah 55:2

Reflection

The spiritual life demands righteousness in order to function as it was designed to function. Righteousness isn't just an ethereal term referring to some intangible halo hovering over certain people. Righteousness is very real. It involves making choices on a regular basis that promote living in accordance with God's will.

The problems come when people search for illegitimate food to feed a legitimate spiritual need for righteousness. This search can include many different things, such as seeking after self-help gurus. While these are not bad in and of themselves, if searching for these things replaces the righteousness of God in your life, that is when they become bad.

Satan is very clever in how he seeks to deceive believers into thinking they are truly consuming spiritual food and righteousness. The Bible says one way he does this is through spiritual teachers who only deliver messages that aim to tickle the ears of the hearers (see 2 Timothy 4:3). But tickling your ears spiritually does not translate into hungering and thirsting after righteousness. That translates more into entertainment. Satan doesn't mind at all if religious sayings or speakers entertain you, because he knows there is no power in religious entertainment. The power comes through tapping into spiritual authority, which can only be done by aligning your heart, thoughts, words, and actions under the truth of God's Word.

Action

1. What are some elements of righteous living that do not often show up in messages or books meant to merely tickle the ears?
2. Name one way you can encourage others to pursue righteousness consistently in their lives.

Prayer

Jesus, I want to honor You by being a greater example of someone who seeks after righteousness and lives in a right relationship with You. Please open doors for me to encourage others to live righteous lives. I pray this in Your name, amen.

Brethren, join in following my example, and observe those who walk according to the pattern you have in us.

Philippians 3:17

Reflection

You are an influencer of your friends, whether you know it or not. That means you have a responsibility to help guide other young men in the faith as well. We must grab hold of those who need to be shown a better way, rather than write them off. Paul told Timothy and others in his sphere of influence that they were to follow his example as he followed Christ (see 1 Corinthians 11:1 and Philippians 3:17). Keep in mind that to have an example to follow means you must have someone setting one. This requires living in a spiritually mature manner and guiding others in how to do likewise. It takes both: ongoing personal discipline and intentional investment in others.

While many are waiting on God to fix what is wrong, He is waiting on young men of faith to step up and do what is right. He is waiting on men who don't just talk about faith but also walk in it. These are the men whose actions demonstrate that they truly believe in the God they claim to worship.

One way to do this is through intentional investments in relationships as well as mutual learning in a spiritual context. The more formal term for this is *discipleship*. We are to live as kingdom disciples pursuing the making of more kingdom disciples throughout our communities, our nation, and the world.

A kingdom disciple can be defined as a believer who takes part in the spiritual development of progressively learning to live all of life under the lordship of Jesus Christ and then seeks to replicate that process in others. As this is done, God's kingdom agenda marches forward on earth.

Action

1. Write out the definition of a kingdom disciple and post it somewhere you can look at it over the next week. Seek to memorize this definition.

2. In what ways can you seek to replicate the process of discipleship in others?

3. Why is it important to disciple others?

Prayer

Jesus, motivate my heart to follow You more closely and to replicate Your will and ways in those around me. Inspire me to be more intentional about impacting others for good and for Your glory. Encourage me by allowing me to see the fruit of this impact when and where I can. In Your name, amen.

Roam to and fro through the streets of Jerusalem,
And look now and take note.
And seek in her open squares,
If you can find a man,
If there is one who does justice, who seeks truth,
Then I will pardon her.

Jeremiah 5:1

Reflection

Over and over God has called men to intervene on behalf of a dying land. Ezekiel 22:30 records it this way, "I searched for a man among them who would build up the wall and stand in the gap before Me for the land, so that I would not destroy it; but I found no one." The land had plenty of males, but God couldn't find a kingdom man. There's a big difference between being a male and being a kingdom man. You can be the former without being the latter when you refuse to take responsibility under God.

Taking responsibility means owning the issues that show up in your life and in the lives of your loved ones. It starts by removing the word *blame* from your vocabulary. No matter who is at fault, it is your role to fix it. That's what a kingdom man does. To blame someone else only leads to bitterness. Bitterness then gives birth to other sins like anger, resentment, and even betrayal.

God is searching for men who will stand in the gap for their friends and communities. Standing in the gap requires courage.

It requires personal responsibility. It requires a removal of blame, finger-pointing, and a victim mentality. Once we put these mindsets aside, we are better positioned to create favorable outcomes for ourselves and for those we love and shepherd.

Action

1. If God were to search our nation today for young men who would stand in the gap so He would not destroy us, how many do you think He would find?
2. How can you become someone God would consider as one who "does justice" and who "seeks truth"?
3. What does it look like in everyday life to do justice or to seek truth?

Prayer

Jesus, help me gain a better understanding of what it means to do justice and seek truth according to Your Word. I want to be a kingdom man who stands in the gap and whom You call on to intervene for our land. Open my heart and train my ears to hear You more clearly so I can live for You and Your kingdom agenda. In Your name, amen.

For that man ought not to expect that he will receive anything from the Lord, being a double-minded man, unstable in all his ways.

James 1:7–8

Reflection

In order to awaken to your full potential, you have to start on a solid foundation based on the Word of God. That means more than just knowing, studying, and memorizing His Word. You have to act on it. The power of His promises remains dormant unless activated by your faith through what you do. Your foundation determines your future.

Your foundation is the Word of God *applied*. It's not just the Word of God *known*. You will not see the intervention of God until He sees your obedience to His truth. God is waiting on you to take your rightful place in this world. He is waiting for you to rise to the occasion and secure your spot of significance in His kingdom made manifest on earth. But that only happens when you step out—fully, faithfully, and single-mindedly—according to the direction of His will.

I'm not suggesting that following God will keep you from the storm. Sometimes when you follow Him, like the disciples who sailed straight into the monstrous storm on the Sea of Galilee, He will direct you into the eye of the storm. But what I am saying is that when you choose to live life by His truth, you will engage the programming of His Word and witness His work in the midst of the storm. The wise man in the parable in Matthew 7:24–29 faced the storm. He didn't avoid the hurricane that came his way. But he withstood it. He didn't succumb to it because he had built his life on the right foundation.

Action

1. What does being a "double-minded" man mean to you?
2. Have you ever known someone who was double-minded, and if so, what were some of the consequences of that in their life?
3. In what ways does our culture seek to make men double-minded?

Prayer

Jesus, I do not want to live as a double-minded man. I want to live as a kingdom man, making my decisions and carrying out my actions based on the truth of Your Word. Show me the way I should go in order to withstand all of life's storms. In Your name, amen.

Do not be deceived, God is not mocked; for whatever a man sows, this he will also reap. For the one who sows to his own flesh will from the flesh reap corruption, but the one who sows to the Spirit will from the Spirit reap eternal life.

Galatians 6:7–8

Reflection

Many young men do not envision success as it really is. They envision it all culminating in fireworks, glitz, and one big resounding stadium of applause. Our entertainment industry and social media sites, along with professional sports, have created this unrealistic view of what it means to be a successful man. Unfortunately, this expectation often causes men to miss out on true success when it comes along. Or it causes them to miss out on enjoying the success they have achieved. As a result of not recognizing it, they wind up chasing the next big thing. And then the next. And the next—always spinning their wheels in the rat race of this temporal life.

Unless we realize what true success looks like and recognize what spiritual success is (which we will explore on Day 40), we may wind up on a never-ending quest for something we've already obtained. Without a clear understanding of kingdom success, we won't know what to invest in with our time, talents, and treasures. Whatever a man sows will be what he reaps. But Satan often gets young men to sow into the wrong things because of this misunderstanding of authentic success.

Action

1. Identify the top three things or visions you have sown into over the last few years and examine any results.
2. Do these results live up to your hopes and expectations? Why or why not?
3. In what ways can you better sow into eternal and authentic visions of kingdom success?

Prayer

Jesus, help me to be mindful of my time and what I choose to invest in. Help me to have an authentic understanding of kingdom success so I do not end up chasing after the wind. Show me what is a waste of my time and what is a valuable thing to focus on or enjoy. In Your name, amen.

This book of the law shall not depart from your mouth, but you shall meditate on it day and night, so that you may be careful to do according to all that is written in it; for then you will make your way prosperous, and then you will have success.

Joshua 1:8

Reflection

Spiritually, success is fulfilling God's purpose for your life. The biblical definition of success means living out your God-given purpose. In our culture today, there are a number of errant descriptions of what it means to be successful. Some people assume that success is tied to how much money a person has. Others base it on how high up the career ladder you go. More and more these days, success is defined by how many followers you have on social media or how many likes you get. But the problem with all these assumptions is that they are not based on God's standard of success.

Jesus gave us the definition of success when He said, "I glorified You on the earth, having accomplished the work which You have given Me to do" (John 17:4).

Paul said the same thing in a different way when he penned these words: "I have fought the good fight, I have finished the course, I have kept the faith" (2 Timothy 4:7).

In fact, God told Joshua that his success was entirely based on his careful meditation on the Word of God combined with aligning his decisions and actions underneath it (see Joshua 1:8). Success involves fulfilling what God has called you to do.

Action

1. What is your personal description of success?
2. What would your life look like, practically and tangibly, for you to consider yourself successful?
3. What do you think is God's definition of success?

Prayer

Jesus, help me to glorify You on earth as You glorified the Father during Your time here. Redefine for me what it means to be successful if my definition differs from Yours at all. Help me to discover the secret of being appreciative of the successes I have accomplished already. In Your name, amen.

I testify to everyone who hears the words of the prophecy of this book: if anyone adds to them, God will add to him the plagues which are written in this book.

Revelation 22:18

Reflection

We read Jesus' words in Matthew 5:18, "For truly I say to you, until heaven and earth pass away, not the smallest letter or stroke shall pass from the Law until all is accomplished." The "letter or stroke" Jesus refers to are the smallest markings in the Hebrew alphabet. He tells us that the Scripture is so complete, comprehensive, and true that the tiniest strokes of it will be fulfilled—every last detail.

Until we discover our need to turn to the truth of God's Word over the lies of the world, we will continue to experience the chaos and confusion that currently engulf us. Jesus told us clearly in John 8:31 that those who abide in the truth of His words are truly His disciples. If you flip that, it makes it clear that when you do not abide in Christ's Word and align under the truth, you are not a kingdom disciple. To abide means to hang out, stay, or remain in. For example, you abide in your home. You live there. To abide in the truth of Christ, you need to live with His perspective. You need to live according to His worldview. It means to live with a desire to know what Jesus feels, thinks, and says on the subject you are dealing with.

You cannot be His disciple and ignore His Word. You cannot be His disciple and reject His Word. You can't say you are a kingdom disciple yet not hold God's Word in high esteem. The two are mutually exclusive.

Action

1. Describe what it means to you in contemporary and practical terms to abide in God's Word.
2. How do you think abiding in God's Word positively impacts your life?

Prayer

Jesus, forgive me for having pulled back from Your Word and failing to abide in it as I should. Your Word is a light to my path. Help me not to stumble in darkness any longer, but to walk according to the truth laid out for me in Your Word. In Your name I pray, amen.

The Light shines in the darkness, and the darkness did not comprehend it. . . . And the Word became flesh, and dwelt among us, and we saw His glory, glory as of the only begotten from the Father, full of grace and truth.

John 1:5, 14

Reflection

Jesus came to give us the truth. In Him is the truth. He is truth. This is why Satan and his demons have tried so hard throughout time to get rid of Jesus or marginalize Him. The light of Christ shines so brightly that darkness has to flee. So instead of taking on a battle they know they will lose, demons seek to deceive people so they never even have a chance to see Christ's light in their lives.

To do this, demons have a school in which most of humanity has enrolled over the years. Scripture calls what they teach there the "doctrines of demons" (1 Timothy 4:1). Satan and his demonic forces seek to trick people with half-truths, partial truths, and all-out lies in order to deceive and control the population. I would imagine that there is not one person reading this book who has not been duped by the devil at one time or another. Satan is the father of lies, and he's a master at deception, particularly those deceits cloaked in partial truths. It's far easier to swallow a lie coated in truth than it is without it. The devil knows that is so, which is why you'll often find truth mixed in with lies when he sets out to deceive (Genesis 3:1–6; Matthew 4:1–11).

When you or anyone else disagree with God, then you are wrong. They are wrong. It is impossible for God to be wrong. God is truth. There are two answers to every question—God's answer and everybody else's. And when everybody else disagrees with God, then everybody else is wrong. When you are the One who made it all to begin with and sustains it all in every moment, you can't be wrong. Jesus, as a part of the triune Godhead, came "full of grace and truth" (John 1:14).

Action

1. What is something Satan deceived you about that impacted your life in a negative way?
2. What did you learn through that experience?
3. How does Jesus' light drive out the darkness of deceit, in practical terms?

Prayer

Jesus, flood my soul with the light of Your truth so that I will know which way to go in my life to live out my kingdom purpose. Forgive me for those times when I not only believed the devil's lies but also promoted them through what I did or said. Cover me with Your goodness and grace so that I can walk confidently in the light of Your Word. In Your name I pray, amen.

The secret of the LORD is for those who fear Him,
And He will make them know His covenant.

Psalm 25:14

Reflection

Everyone wants to be a success. Nobody sets out to fail. And while none of us can go back and undo the mistakes of yesteryears, each of us has the option of becoming successful from here on out. We can begin the journey or continue the journey of fulfilling God's destiny for us as young men.

God gives us the secret to living a life of success in Psalm 25:14. To know God's covenant is to know His favor and His blessings, as God's covenant is expressly tied to His covering. Align yourself under God's relational, covenantal rule in life, and you will experience spiritual success.

But there is a condition to success that this secret reveals to us if you look at it closely enough. This condition is that you only get to know God's covenant by fearing Him. There exists a cause-and-effect scenario for achieving spiritual success. The amount of honor and respect you have for God and His Word will directly impact your level of spiritual success. You can't dishonor God in your decisions and expect to achieve any level of kingdom success. God has a standard, and He does not adjust that standard to cultural norms.

Action

1. What does the term *covenant* mean to you?
2. Describe how you feel about living your life in alignment with God's covenant.
3. What areas of your life need to be adjusted to show God a greater level of respect?

Prayer

Jesus, show me where I am dishonoring You with decisions that are made outside of Your covenant so that I can adjust and get in alignment with You. Help me to move forward in spiritual success through the choices I make. In Your name, amen.

The fear of the Lord prolongs life,
But the years of the wicked will be shortened.

Proverbs 10:27

Reflection

Driving has become a normal way of getting around. But have
you ever stopped to think of the power of a car? Without going
into the minutia of physics, let me give a fairly simple example.
It's been stated that if you crash your car while driving at 65 miles
per hour, it is the same force you would face if you drove your car
off a twelve-story building.[1]

Now, most of us driving a car on top of a twelve-story building would be extremely careful. Yet many of us casually driving
down the highway at 65 miles per hour have been known to let
our minds wander. The reason we pay more attention on top of the
building is that we can see the potential result should we drive off
the edge. So we take our driving up there seriously. But since we
have become so used to driving on highways at 65 miles per hour,
many of us don't consider how dangerous it really is. As soon as
you take your attention off the road, where it needs to be, a crash
can loudly declare, "Game over."

There are boundaries around the use of a high-powered vehicle.
And those boundaries are honored through what we do. If you

learned to drive, I'm sure someone told you to honor those rules and regulations. We take driving seriously.

Yet far too many young men understand how to take driving seriously but have no clue how to do the same with God. They want the benefits of God without the boundaries that a proper fear and awe of Him create. They treat God like the cop they see in the rearview mirror. He affects what you do when He's in visible proximity—perhaps in church or a small-group setting. But get outside of cultural Christianity, and the foot presses hard on the accelerator once again.

Action

1. What are some consequences for failing to fear God?
2. Have you experienced any of these consequences, or similar ones, in your life? If yes, what did you learn?
3. How can we encourage others in our lives to take God more seriously?

Prayer

Jesus, Your boundaries are there to preserve and protect me. They are not there to cause me harm. Help me to remember this truth so that I will honor the boundaries You have set in place rather than dismiss them. In Your name, amen.

Be anxious for nothing, but in everything by prayer and supplication with thanksgiving let your requests be made known to God. And the peace of God, which surpasses all comprehension, will guard your hearts and your minds in Christ Jesus.

Philippians 4:6–7

Reflection

An article was published not too long ago that said Americans had purchased over 300 million prescriptions for antidepressants in 2021 alone.[1] That was a sharp increase from the year before and a definite sign of the times. It is clear people are struggling with mental health as we witness the restlessness all around. One of the reasons indicated was a lack of satisfaction with life as it was. And while there is a place for assistance when you need it, God's Word also provides a way to help with calming your heart and emotions.

Satisfaction is yours for the taking. It's as simple as conforming your thoughts and your actions to the will of God. Much of the disenchantment and despondency we face week after week or month after month is tied to famished souls. Our souls are starving because we have relegated God to the status of a social media influencer instead of esteeming Him and His rule as first and foremost.

God doesn't just want to influence you. He—as God—is in charge. He is the ultimate Ruler, and He rules over all. In order to rightly align under Him, you will need to consistently feed your soul by exposing your mind to righteous thoughts, righteous words, and righteous behavior.

And if you're not used to feeding on so much righteousness at one time, then start where you can. Set down your cell phone and pick up your Bible. Turn off the television and read a book or listen to a podcast on righteousness-based principles. As your soul expands with the righteousness of God, your hunger and your thirst will grow also, in order to meet the growing appetite of your soul.

Action

1. Why do you think there is an increase in the number of people depending on outside help for mental wellness?
2. In what ways can a firm faith in God and His Word help bring calm and satisfaction?

Prayer

Jesus, help me understand what I need to do to live my life in a state of harmony, satisfaction, and peace. I love You and want to know You more. In Your name I pray, amen.

For all have sinned and fall short of the glory of God.

Romans 3:23

Reflection

What would you say to a basketball player who kept running toward the wrong basket while dribbling the ball? You'd probably tell him to go sit down. As a coach, you wouldn't have time for that.

Thankfully, God doesn't exist in time like we do, and He's not bound by linear limitations as we are. He's got all the time in the world—and then some. And He doesn't just kick us off the team for running in the wrong direction. God grasps that none of us is perfect and we all fall short (Romans 3:23). Yet that doesn't make our rebellion any less serious than it is. God's patience doesn't translate into a free pass to keep going our own way. God's patience translates into more time for us to grow.

If you have found yourself heading in the wrong direction—by what you think, say, or do—turn around. There's no time like the present to get back into alignment with God. God wants you to follow Him. He doesn't want to see you suffer the consequences of living apart from Him and His rule over your life.

Action

1. Describe a moment when you knew you were headed in the wrong direction.
2. What did you choose to do about it?
3. Looking back, in what ways are you happy or disappointed with the choices you made?

Prayer

Jesus, You are full of forgiveness for those who seek You. I want to experience Your forgiveness for anything that I have done that has taken me outside of Your covenantal will for my life. Give me grace and mercy to get back on the right track with You. In Your name, amen.

After He had removed him, He raised up David to be their king, concerning whom He also testified and said, "I HAVE FOUND DAVID the son of Jesse, A MAN AFTER MY HEART, who will do all My will."

Acts 13:22

Reflection

King David became a successful warrior even though he grew up herding sheep, skipping rocks, and playing instruments. David didn't attend military school. But he knew the One in charge. And because of that, David won his battles and his wars (see 1 Chronicles 18:1). A critical aspect of David's military leadership and victory came through his awareness of and willingness to seek God's guidance. No other biblical narrative contains more inquiries of God than David's. Each time he asked to know God's will and God's ways, he got an answer.

As a result, David stood strongly positioned to annihilate his enemies and redeem his people from certain death. David, a kingdom man after God's own heart, understood the value of this treasure called guidance. He feared God, which enabled him to follow God more fully.

Life is full of choices. The problem with many of our decisions is that we cannot see what's coming up next. It's like being on a highway that is twisting and turning, and you are unable to see around the next bend. You have to slow down because you don't know where you're going. Life is filled with unknowns. But that's why David prayed a prayer that all young men should pray: "Make me know Your ways, O Lord; teach me Your paths" (Psalm 25:4). That's not just a sweet verse to say on Sunday. That's a plea for a game plan. It's a cry to know the next call.

Action

1. When you reach a decision point, how will you go to God first rather than try to figure it out yourself?
2. In what way was David a better man by always going to God for direction?
3. What are some things that cause men to hesitate to go to God for direction?

Prayer

Jesus, slow down my thinking enough that I have time to discern when I need to go to God for direction. Help me not to get so caught up in being busy that I forget where wisdom comes from. In Your name, amen.

For bodily discipline is only of little profit, but godliness is profitable for all things, since it holds promise for the present life and also for the life to come.

1 Timothy 4:8

Reflection

One of the greatest challenges in our culture today is the sheer difficulty of calling young men to strive for biblical manhood. It seems that simply taking responsibility for your thoughts and actions has become a lost art. We might be facing a worldwide plague of personal irresponsibility and entitlement. And that just doesn't cut it in the long run.

Imagine if a football coach drafted a star running back with all the potential in the world. He had speed. Moves. Balance. Intuition to read the opposition. All of that and more. On paper, he was amazing. But when he showed up to practice, he just sat down the whole time.

If the coach told him to get on the field to practice, he'd just shrug it off and say he didn't feel like it. Or that he was busy. Or any other excuse that came to mind. Then on game day, when he failed to make the plays or score the points and the coach asked him why he didn't accomplish the goals of the game, the player blamed the opposition. Or, worse yet, he blamed his teammates.

This player wouldn't last long on any team, regardless of his stats, strength, and size when they drafted him. Unleashing a powerful running back requires more than potential and natural ability. It requires intentionality, practice, and responsibility. Achieving biblical manhood requires no less.

Action

1. What would the common response be to the coach who cut the player who didn't exert himself or practice?
2. Why do we often judge God when He chooses not to participate in or bless the lives of men who do not actively pursue Him?
3. Describe what personal spiritual responsibility means to you.

Prayer

Jesus, applying spiritual responsibility in my life requires effort and a heart to seek You in all I do. Help me to break free from the bonds of laziness so I can experience You more fully. In Your name, amen.

When Jesus saw him lying there, and knew that he had already been a long time in that condition, He said to him, "Do you wish to get well?"

John 5:6

Reflection

To unleash the full potential of who you are as a young man of God, you'll need to first make sure you're up for the challenge. Manning up starts by standing up. If you do not take the divinely ordained responsibility that God has given to you and every man, by virtue of His purpose when He made you, then you are wasting your life. Even with fineries decorating his home, office, or social media sites—an irresponsible man is no kingdom man at all.

Healing and empowerment are not a one-way gift bestowed with a magic wand. To be unleashed in your fullest potential requires your desire, responsibility, and focus. That's why Jesus would often ask the question "Do you want to be made well?" He didn't just walk around tapping people on the head, bestowing health and power on whoever was near. Rather, Jesus would ask if the person was willing to be made whole. He didn't want to force healing on them because he wanted to reach deeper than just their physical needs. You don't light a candle by putting a flame to the outer wax. You have to light the wick.

You also don't place a candle out in direct sunlight, not if you don't want to waste it. But far too many men are content with being like the flicker of a candle under the noonday sun. Unnoticed. Having no impact. Making no mark on a world that desperately needs godly young men to carry their light into the dark corners where it is most needed.

Action

1. What parts of you need to be made well, whether physically, emotionally, or spiritually?
2. How have you expressed this desire to Jesus?
3. What improvements in your life has Jesus been free to make over the last year?

Prayer

Jesus, I want to be whole and healed of anything that keeps me from fully living out my purpose in Your kingdom plan. Help me to overcome my addictions and propensities that draw me away from You. In Your name, amen.

Blessed are the merciful, for they shall receive mercy.

Matthew 5:7

Reflection

"Lord, have mercy!" It's a phrase many, if not most of us, have uttered at some time or another. Sometimes we've said it jokingly. Other times we've said it with full sincerity. It is a cry to God for His mercy, help, and intervention in what seems like a deep pit and a dark hole. But did you know that mercy comes tied to your actions? The mercy God extends to you is often tied to your own actions toward others. You can actually increase the level of mercy God shows to you by increasing the level of mercy you show to others. That's why it's such an important part of living the successful kingdom life.

Mercy involves compassion, kindness, hope, and help. Mercy is so important that Jesus included it in His Sermon on the Mount. He called it out as a foundational value.

Jesus called attention to those who extend care and compassion to others when He pointed out how important mercy truly is. He said, "Blessed are the merciful, for they shall receive mercy" (Matthew 5:7). To understand what it means to live with this value of being merciful, we need to first understand mercy.

Mercy can be defined as compassion for someone in need. It involves reducing, removing, or relieving someone's distress.

Scripture tells us that our salvation is a result of mercy. We read in Titus 3:5, "He saved us, not on the basis of deeds which we have done in righteousness, but according to His mercy, by the washing of regeneration and renewing by the Holy Spirit."

In fact, mercy summarizes God's reaction to our individual misery (Psalm 130:1–8). It involves more than feeling sorry for someone. Mercy means the sorrow you feel for someone else shows up in your actions done out of an intention to help relieve their pain. Mercy always involves an action that seeks to reduce or remove the misery that has come about in someone else's life.

Action

1. What is one way you have shown someone mercy?
2. How have you experienced God's mercy in your own life?
3. Define in your own terms what it means to be merciful.

Prayer

Jesus, I want to be a person who not only experiences God's mercy readily in my life, but who shows others mercy also. In Your name I pray, amen.

The LORD is good to all,
And His mercies are over all His works.

Psalm 145:9

Reflection

God's mercy serves as an illustration for how we are to be merciful to others. Mercy isn't contingent on what someone else can do. And it doesn't depend on whether the other person deserves it. If we needed to earn the air we breathe or the sunrise that gives us light, which God so mercifully supplies, none of us would be here. Mercy presupposes that the person receiving it is not entitled to what he or she is receiving.

Thus, when you show someone mercy, it's not a favor. It's not a business transaction. It's not quid pro quo. Mercy provides relief from sorrow and pronounces a state of well-being on the recipient, regardless of what they have done up to that point.

There are two common reasons people need mercy. One is the debilitating impact of sin in their lives. The other is the painful weight of circumstances that have arisen through no fault of their own. Yet regardless of the cause of the suffering, mercy extends relief to those who need it, whether or not you agree with them and what they have done in their lives.

God wants us to set aside our own selfishness and our own pain or historical wounds in order to show kindness and mercy to whoever needs it most. We often use the trauma of the past as an excuse to live angry and bitter lives today, feeling that somehow means we are pursuing justice. But God reminds us that true justice shows up when we show mercy. This is because it is only when we overcome the evil of hate in our own hearts by showing mercy to those around us that God is freed up to show us mercy as well.

Action

1. How different would this world be if there were more people showing mercy than fighting for their own rights and revenge?
2. What steps can you take to distance yourself from the cultural hate and anger so prevalent in our world today, as well as judgment toward other groups of people?

Prayer

Jesus, free me from the need to always be right or to withhold love from those I do not feel deserve it. Show me what a blessing it is to me when I show mercy to others, especially to those I do not feel deserve it. I love You and am grateful for the mercy You show me every day. In Your name I pray, amen.

Two men went up into the temple to pray, one a Pharisee and the other a tax collector. The Pharisee stood and was praying this to himself: "God, I thank You that I am not like other people: swindlers, unjust, adulterers, or even like this tax collector. I fast twice a week; I pay tithes of all that I get." But the tax collector, standing some distance away, was even unwilling to lift up his eyes to heaven, but was beating his breast, saying, "God, be merciful to me, the sinner!" I tell you, this man went to his house justified rather than the other; for everyone who exalts himself will be humbled, but he who humbles himself will be exalted.

Luke 18:10–14

Reflection

Have you ever looked around you, like the Pharisee did, and inwardly thanked God that you are not like the others? It's okay to admit it if you have. Admitting it is the first step to repentance and getting right with God. This kind of spirit, which causes us to feel better than others, keeps us distant from God.

As we saw in the passage for today, the Pharisee was confident he was doing all the right things. His heart was rooted in pride. But the tax collector knew he needed help. He knew he made mistakes and committed sins. Jesus made it clear to us through this parable that the one who asked for mercy out of a heart of humility received the mercy he needed. Jesus also emphasized that the Pharisee who had exalted himself would at some point be humbled. He would someday find himself in a position that made him realize he needed mercy. But by then, without a change of heart, it might be too late to access it.

Similarly, when you and I go through our lives with a heart of pride and a lack of willingness to address our sins that are creating the misery and chaos that consume us, we will neither show others mercy nor will we receive any for ourselves. Yet we can rest assured that there will come a day when we will know how much we need it.

Action

1. Which of the two men in the parable do you most identify with and why?
2. Why do you think God responded favorably to the tax collector and not the Pharisee?

Prayer

Jesus, forgive me, for I am a sinner. I humbly bow before You and ask that You will forgive any and all pride that rises in my heart causing me to believe I am better than anyone else You have created. In Your name I pray, amen.

I am the vine, you are the branches; he who abides in Me and I in him, he bears much fruit, for apart from Me you can do nothing.

John 15:5

Reflection

You are free to get over whatever it is that has gripped you as soon as you decide to do just that. How long you've been bound doesn't matter. How deep the addiction runs doesn't matter. You can get up. You can get over the obstacles that keep you down.

God frequently uses broken people to accomplish His kingdom agenda on earth. Time after time in Scripture, we read about the broken people God raised up in powerful ways. He used Moses, a murderer, to deliver the Hebrew slaves. He used Jacob, a liar and a trickster, to fulfill His promise to Abraham. He even used Peter after his denial, Solomon after his idolatry, and Samson after his multiple failures. If God redeemed their lives, He can redeem your life too.

Brokenness should never keep you bound. A broken past should never limit a bright future. Rather, it should release you into a greater life of purpose through what you have learned, because a truly broken person understands the reality of John 15:5, where Jesus says, "Apart from Me you can do nothing." A broken man who has learned both surrender to and dependence on God is a force to be reckoned with.

Action

1. What is your vision for how you want God to use you in the future?
2. How can you participate in the fulfillment of this vision?
3. What hesitations do you have about participating?

Prayer

Jesus, show me Your plans for me and how You want to go about bringing these plans to fruition. Help me to understand Your purpose for my life so that I can participate with You in living it out. In Your name, amen.

So that at the name of Jesus EVERY KNEE WILL BOW, of those who are in heaven and on earth and under the earth.

Philippians 2:10

Reflection

In the Bible, names matter. Names have meanings. Names are never mere nomenclature. People weren't named because it sounded nice, or their parents were copying a celebrity somewhere, or their mom suggested it—*strongly*. Names carried weight and character and were often tied to the future. That's why, throughout Scripture, when God was about to do something new in a place or with a person, He would often change the name.

Abram became Abraham.
Jacob became Israel.
Simon became Peter.

All through the Bible, God is switching around names because He's switching up identities or purposes tied to His kingdom roles. A person was given a new name designed to fit the reputation or character of his or her new path. Names held power tied to purpose.

The name of Jesus, of course, held—and holds—the power above all power.

It's time to own your life through a proper understanding and use of the power of the name of Jesus. It's time to take charge of who you are by identifying with and in Him. Stop letting other people's thoughts, words, or actions drive you down. There is power in the name of Jesus, no matter the circumstance. Because in His name, you can get up and send your opposition flying while unleashing your full potential.

Action

1. What does your name mean?
2. Why do you think God wanted you to have that name?

Prayer

Jesus, give me a greater understanding and awareness of what my purpose is in life so that I can fulfill the plans You have for me. Help me to identify my calling and live up to the name You have chosen for me on this journey. In Your name, amen.

Remember me for this, O my God, and do not blot out my loyal deeds which I have performed for the house of my God and its services.

Nehemiah 13:14

Reflection

If you want God to relieve your burdens and lighten your load, you need to stop skipping over the opportunities He gives you to do the same for others around you. Nehemiah is a perfect example of this in the Bible. Throughout the book, we see Nehemiah doing good to those in need. He had a comfortable position in a comfortable location with a comfortable outlook on life. After all, He was the cupbearer to the king of Persia. But despite his comfort, Nehemiah's heart became burdened for his people, the Israelites. His heart became broken over the plight of Jerusalem.

So, in the book named after him, we see Nehemiah leaving the comfort of his surroundings and going out to help people who are hurting. He leads the campaign to rebuild the walls of Jerusalem. He brings justice to a group of people who were being treated unjustly. He feeds and clothes people who need it, and he supplies and enables them to defend themselves, their families, and the city.

Yet as you read through the struggles and difficulties Nehemiah had to overcome to bring about such good for others, you see a repeated phrase. It's a short phrase, and you may have missed it if you read the chapters quickly. But twice in the book, you will find "Remember me, O my God, for good" (Nehemiah 5:19 and 13:31).

As Nehemiah is doing good for others and showing mercy to those in need, he is looking up to God in heaven and nudging Him with this phrase. In other words, He is asking God to take note. Nehemiah prayed this way because he knew the kingdom principle that giving sets you up to receive. That's what the Bible means when it says you are more blessed to give than to receive (Acts 20:35).

Action

1. Have you ever asked God to specifically remember the good and merciful things you have done for others when asking Him to show mercy to you? If so, what was the result?

2. Have you been encouraged by helping someone else? If so, how did that impact your desire to help others more?

Prayer

Jesus, remember me for good when You think of my life and the things that I need regarding Your mercy, comfort, and care. Remember the times that no one else even noticed, but You did. In Your name I pray, amen.

Your word is a lamp to my feet
And a light to my path.

Psalm 119:105

Reflection

One day I was in my car and the side mirror had collapsed. I couldn't get it to open back up to where it was supposed to be. So I decided to figure it out. I fiddled with that mirror, pushed that mirror, pulled that mirror, and sought to maneuver that mirror for close to twenty minutes.

Eventually, it dawned on me that in the glove box of my car was a book, the car owner's manual. Now, honestly speaking, I hadn't opened that book before, even though I owned it. Until I was stuck. So this time, I grabbed the book. It didn't take me too long to figure out how to fix my mirror once I decided to use the book designed exactly for that purpose—to help me operate my car.

A lot of us will pick up the Bible and put it on the side table or by our bed. But we fail to open it to see what is inside—to read, discern, learn, and be impacted by its truth. Yet when we fail to treat Scripture as the absolute, inerrant, authoritative voice of God in print, it is we who will pay the price, in our lives, relationships, schooling, finances, peace of mind, and so much more. The things that plague us will only increase when we neglect to learn and apply God's truth to the situations and challenges we face.

Many believers today are wasting a lot of time and experiencing a lot of frustration because they refuse to go to the one place that holds the answers to any problems they face. If they, or we as the body of Christ, would simply return to *the* source of truth as *our* source of truth and then do what it says, we could solve the issues creating the chaos around us and within us.

Action

1. What does it mean to you personally to "return to *the* source of truth as *our* source of truth"?

2. In what areas would you like to see God give you greater grace or favor in your life?

Prayer

Jesus, reveal to me the ways to please You. Help me to always stay close to Your Word so that I can stand on the foundation of knowing what truth is. I don't want to be deceived by culture, friends, or family members, so give me a greater level of discernment to spot the lies and inconsistencies in what I'm hearing all around me. In Your name I pray, amen.

And we also thank God continually because, when you received the word of God, which you heard from us, you accepted it not as a human word, but as it actually is, the word of God, which is indeed at work in you who believe.

1 Thessalonians 2:13 NIV

Reflection

In order for the word of truth to work in building kingdom virtue in our lives, we must allow humility to enter our hearts in such a way that we understand God is the author of truth, and we are not. When we don't do that, it doesn't stop the truth from being the truth. It just changes the power of the truth in how it works for us.

When we talk about receiving the truth, keep in mind that it's the truth of God that you need to receive. It doesn't necessarily mean what a preacher said, or even a biblical scholar, or what was printed in a Christian magazine. Many people peddle the Word out of a wrong motivation or are simply misguided themselves, though their motives may be pure.

Paul urged Timothy to stick with the truth in 2 Timothy 4:1–5. Just as there are today, there were people in Paul's day seeking to say what "itching ears" want to hear. Good-sounding, popular myths fill pulpits all across our nation because so many people have abandoned the truth. Far too many people simply want to be placated. They want to be made to feel good. They want a doughnut sermon—one that satisfies the taste buds but has no nutritional value.

If you will look to God's Word for teaching, correction, and direction, you will know how to navigate the challenges and chaos of this world. The Bible is our control tower. It is our source of all truth.

Action

1. When you read the Bible, do you tend to go to those passages that support what you are already thinking? How do you respond to the passages that convict you or disagree with your thoughts?

2. Is there an idea or construct within you that God's Word continually seeks to convict and correct? If so, what is it, and are you open to yielding it to the truth?

3. Ask God to intervene in your heart and mind and reveal areas where you need the light of His Word to guide you.

Prayer

Father, I believe Your Word is true, but sometimes I avoid it. Or at least, I avoid those places in it that convict me of wrong thoughts or wrong actions. Forgive me for distancing Your Word from my life so that I don't have to do the uncomfortable work of changing my life to align all of it under You. Thank You for the grace of Your forgiveness. In Jesus' name, amen.

For whatever is born of God overcomes the world; and this is the victory that has overcome the world—our faith.

1 John 5:4

Reflection

Perhaps you didn't have a good beginning upon which to build. Maybe your parents fought or divorced early on. Maybe you didn't come from a nice neighborhood or a school system whose funding indicated that your future was taken seriously. Maybe you had to raise yourself because your mom worked three jobs. Or maybe you lived in the suburbs, but you were abused, neglected, or pacified with stuff. You were kept busy to keep you away from any real relationship at home. Whatever the case, where you start doesn't determine where you are going. Jesus started out in an obscure town named Nazareth, after all.

Since Jesus came from such a no-name place, He can meet any man in any place at any time, even when your life seems worthless. He can turn it around and set you on your feet, if you will just look to Jesus from Nazareth. Look to Jesus even if you feel you're in a place with no hope, no opportunity, and no way out.

The truth of this reality strips young men of any excuses they might have claimed, such as, "If it weren't for her," or "If it weren't for them," or "If it weren't for that circumstance, or my background, or my limitations." Yes, all those circumstances can be real. But in the name of Jesus Christ, the one from *Nazareth*, you don't need to be whining anymore. You can get up. You can walk. You can be responsible. You are no longer to see yourself as a victim. Your relationship with Jesus Christ makes you an overcomer (1 John 5:1–4).

Action

1. What is one thing from your past that you need to overcome or let go in order to move forward?
2. What are you willing to do in order to stop blaming that situation or person and move on?
3. Why do you think Jesus wants you to stop the blame game?

Prayer

Jesus, the things that have happened to me in my past were allowed by You. I trust that You had a plan for them. Show me how I can let go of the pain of the past to be set free from a cycle of blame. In Your name, amen.

And they overcame him because of the blood of the Lamb and because of the word of their testimony, and they did not love their life even when faced with death.

Revelation 12:11

Reflection

Suddenly. It's a word you'll hear often in the Bible. One thing you need to understand as you dive deeper into this concept of unleashing biblical manhood is that God doesn't need time. He can do whatever He wants whenever He wants to. He's just waiting for you to look to Him in order to receive a supernatural infusion of His power. The moment you are ready, God is too. When God wants to move, He can move faster than an X-15 rocket plane tearing across the sky at Mach 6.

God wants you whole and strong not just for you. He wants those in your circle of influence to be spiritually healthy and mature too. If all you are doing is participating in church or attending a college ministry or throwing God a prayer here or there, you are not demonstrating to others who God has created you to be.

If and when God transforms any aspect of your life (emotions, addictions, relationships, and more), you've got to make it known. You've got to share this truth with others. Don't be ashamed. Don't be shy. God has given you your testimony for a reason. Don't miss the purpose of the miracle, which is to draw others toward their miracles as quickly as God chooses.

Action

1. Have you ever shared your testimony publicly, and if so, what was the result?
2. Why is it important to tell others what Jesus has done for you?
3. Have you been encouraged by someone else's testimony? If so, how did that impact your life?

Prayer

Jesus, give me a greater level of boldness to share with others the things You have done in my life. I want to be someone who encourages people by telling of the impact You have made both in and through me. In Your name, amen.

And do not be conformed to this world, but be transformed by the renewing of your mind, so that you may prove what the will of God is, that which is good and acceptable and perfect.

Romans 12:2

Reflection

A prisoner of war (POW) is a person who has been captured by the enemy and is held hostage in the context of a conflict. The opposing forces control the prisoner's living conditions, activities, and movements. Many young men live like POWs, but rather than being prisoners of war, they're prisoners of addictive behavior. They have been captured by the enemy, and there appears to be no way of escape.

They feel trapped in situations and circumstances that the world labels as addiction. Drugs, sex, pornography, alcohol, relationships, negative self-talk, food, gambling—these things can become the go-to coping mechanisms for life's pain, disappointments, and boredom. When an action or activity begins to influence you more than you influence it, it can leave you feeling trapped.

Overcoming addictions begins with identifying the root of the problem and addressing it in your mind. Maybe you're dealing with loneliness, depression, past trauma, or something else. Whatever is leading you to addiction, these issues must be addressed for you to fully unleash your biblical manhood. If you don't address them, then addictions will leave their negative impacts through broken relationships, broken bodies, broken dreams, and destroyed lives. It is time to be set free from the symptoms of wrong thinking. It's up to you to get started on the path to wholeness and victory.

Action

1. What is the root of one of the prominent struggles or addictions you face or have faced?
2. What are some ways the root can be extracted or healed in your life?
3. What happens if you seek to treat symptoms of a stronghold rather than the root?

Prayer

Jesus, reveal to me the root at the heart of the struggles I face and the strongholds that seek to consume me. Show me how to address the root and heal from whatever I need to be healed from in order to experience the freedom of Your love. In Your name, amen.

Blessed are the pure in heart, for they shall see God.

Matthew 5:8

Reflection

To see God, who is holy, we need to look toward Him with spiritual eyes. We need to purify our hearts. We are told that we are blessed when we have pure hearts, and we will see God as a result. Many of us are not seeing God for ourselves because we are taking in things that contaminate our spiritual systems. We are allowing in the pollutants of the culture, which then produce watery, itchy spiritual eyes. These cultural contaminants cloud our vision to such a degree that we no longer recognize or experience God's work, power, provision, transformation, deliverance, and victory firsthand.

Spiritually speaking, a pure heart means singleness of devotion. It means to love all of God with all of you, not just a portion of you for a time. Purity of heart means you are no longer disconnected from God by allowing sin to defile your relationship with Him.

God and sin are irreconcilable. He simply can't be comfortable where unrighteousness is allowed to express itself freely. Jesus reminds us in this kingdom value that if we are going to see God at a more intimate level, we must live with a pursuit of purity.

Now, don't misunderstand this. Jesus' concern is about purity— real purity. It's easy to camouflage ourselves so that we look a lot cleaner than we are, but Jesus knows us intimately and can see through the façade. That's why He called the Pharisees out when He said, "Woe to you, scribes and Pharisees, hypocrites! For you clean the outside of the cup and of the dish, but inside they are full of robbery and self-indulgence" (Matthew 23:25).

God is not after a purity of appearance, or a purity of location, or even a purity of religious activity. None of that matters if the heart itself is impure. To see God and recognize His hand in your life and His guidance of your heart, you must purify your heart so that you can dwell near Him, in close proximity relationally.

Action

1. What is one thing you can work on to help purify your heart right now?
2. What happens in your life when you draw close to God and recognize His hand in your life?

Prayer

Jesus, purify my heart to such a degree that I am able to clearly see God and His work in my life. I repent of the sin that contaminates my life. Help me to be pure, Jesus, as You are pure. I pray this in Your name, amen.

You are of your father the devil, and you want to do the desires of your father. He was a murderer from the beginning, and does not stand in the truth because there is no truth in him. Whenever he speaks a lie, he speaks from his own nature, for he is a liar and the father of lies.

John 8:44

Reflection

When you tell yourself, *I can't stop looking at these images*, whose thought is that? Or when you think, *I have to have this drink*, whose thought is that? Or when you entertain thoughts such as *I am nothing. I have no value. I don't have power over my emotions of lust or anger*, who is doing the talking? We know these thoughts come from Satan because they are all lies, and he is the father of lies (John 8:44).

Satan makes quick work of planting and directing thoughts. But his thoughts do not have to have the last word. You have the power to control your own thoughts.

How should you respond to Satan's planted thoughts? The same way Jesus did when Peter tried to keep Him from going to the cross. Peter told Jesus, "God forbid it, Lord! This shall never happen to You." To which Jesus replied, "Get behind Me, Satan!" (Matthew 16:22–23).

The words came from Peter, but the thoughts came from Satan. When Satan gets into your mind, he gets into your actions. The key to overcoming addictive behavior is to take your thoughts captive (see 2 Corinthians 10:5), which we will tackle on Day 66.

Action

1. How can a believer discern between his own thoughts and thoughts planted by Satan?
2. Do you make discernment an active part of your life? If not, will you consider doing so?
3. What do you think are some of Satan's goals in planting thoughts in the minds of Christians?

Prayer

Jesus, give me greater discernment to be able to cut through the lies of Satan and identify Your truth. Help me not to fall into the trap of lies and deception. In Your name, amen.

He who has My commandments and keeps them is the one who loves Me; and he who loves Me will be loved by My Father, and I will love him and will disclose Myself to him.

John 14:21

Reflection

Many of us have water filter systems in our homes. We don't drink the tap water. Instead, we take the water and run it through a filtering system to remove the impurities or toxins in it. This is because we do not want the invisible bacteria, chemicals, and additives to harm our bodies.

The way we feel about our water is the way God feels about our hearts. He knows that the contaminants of sin and the pollutants of pride harm a person's life. He doesn't want to see our hearts impure, not only because that offends Him, but also because He knows how it destroys us. It destroys our relationships and thought processes, and even damages our dreams and destinies. We can no longer see the pristine nature of who God is and what He has placed within us.

A lot of the misery we experience in life is due to our being slaves to what we see. We assume that what we see is all there is to reality because we cannot see from God's perspective. When you live according to the kingdom value of a pure spiritual heart, you will grow to see more through God's eyes. You gain an entrance into His eternal perspective.

How many battles have you gone out to fight that God had already planned to defend you from? Seeing God because you live with this pureness of heart kingdom value gives you the ability to see life spiritually. You can see God's hand steering you away from danger in time. You can see His heart lovingly directing you toward your destiny. You can see the potential pitfalls on the path you've chosen so that you can avoid them. Seeing God means you will see what you need to in order to live your life to the fullest. It is an ability we all need.

Action

1. What is your perspective of God?
2. In what ways can you help yourself see Him more fully?
3. What would you like to see improved in your life through a closer relationship with God?

Prayer

Jesus, help me to see my life and everything that takes place around me through spiritual eyes. Give me eyes to see You, and in doing so, I will see spiritually. In Your name I pray, amen.

Blessed are the peacemakers, for they shall be called sons of God.

Matthew 5:9

Reflection

Whatever the particulars of the conflict and wherever it may appear, it looks like everywhere you turn these days there is war. The same was common in Jesus' day as well.

Peace is harmony where conflict used to exist. But peace is more than a truce. After all, two people or two nations can stop fighting physically but still live in a state of cold war. Some married couples assume they have peace in their relationship because they don't talk to each other. But that is not peace. That's a relational cold war.

To be a peacemaker is to live as someone who does not run away from conflict, but rather faces the conflict with truth in such a way so as to resolve it. A peacemaker is more than a peacekeeper. A peacemaker ought to be able to step back from the former combatants and have them continue to get along because they have experienced a real resolution to the problem.

This is why peace must always be accompanied by righteousness. Psalm 85:10 explains this relationship: "Lovingkindness and truth have met together; righteousness and peace have kissed each other." When love and truth meet, the mouths of righteousness and peace similarly connect, producing the necessary results.

Hebrews 12:14 links peace and righteousness: "Pursue peace with all men, and the sanctification without which no one will see the Lord." We are to pursue peace, but we must remember that this pursuit cannot be absent of sanctification. That is, we could pursue peace, but cannot obtain it without the righteous requirements of God.

To be a peacemaker is to be someone who is actively involved in creating harmony where conflict once existed. For those who choose to intentionally live according to this value, the blessing you will receive is to be "called sons of God."

Action

1. In what ways do you actively pursue peacemaking?
2. What do you think are some of the reasons Satan seeks to disrupt the peace in our world and in believers' lives?

Prayer

Jesus, give me greater discernment to be able to identify when Satan is disrupting the peace. Help me to be aware so that I do not fall into the trap of division and sowing discord among those in my sphere of influence. In Your name I pray, amen.

For a child will be born to us, a son will be given to us;
And the government will rest on His shoulders;
And His name will be called Wonderful Counselor,
    Mighty God,
Eternal Father, Prince of Peace.

Isaiah 9:6

Reflection

Satan's agenda is to create conflict. His aim is to divide. The reason he makes this his overarching goal is because he knows that God is a God of unity. He knows that God is a God of peace. Any time Satan can get believers quarreling or being divisive, he is taking aim at the very heart of God. Satan knows that God does not hang out with division. God does not abide in disunity.

Conflict within families is one of the devil's favorite forms of disunity. He enjoys stirring things up between parents and children as well as between siblings and friends. A favorite pastime of Satan is sowing bitterness, arguing, and confusion in the church. The more he can divide us, the more power he has over us because he has distanced us from the only thing able to overpower him: the kingdom authority of God.

Satan is not after you solely to destroy your emotions or disturb your thoughts. In doing so, he's after everyone else as well. The more people you have with messed-up emotions and destructive thoughts interacting, living together, or working together, the easier it is to keep people divided. And when Satan keeps people apart, he also successfully keeps them from accessing the authority of heaven in a hellish world.

When you and I resort to living as conflict contributors rather than as peacemakers, we have inadvertently chosen sides. We have aligned ourselves with the agenda of the devil. God is a God of harmony and oneness. That doesn't mean we all have to agree all the time or see things the same way, but it does mean that in our disagreements, we express ourselves in a way that demonstrates we are unified toward a common goal—that of advancing God's kingdom agenda on earth.

Action

1. Describe the link between seeking peace and experiencing peace.
2. Why do you think Satan likes to go after your thoughts when trying to disrupt your peace?
3. What practice can you put in place to help you protect and preserve the level of peace you experience in your personal life?

Prayer

Jesus, I want to master my emotions and thoughts to such a degree that I do not give in to Satan's ploys and strategies as he seeks to trip me up. I love You and want to reflect You in all I do. In Your name I pray, amen.

We are destroying speculations and every lofty thing raised up against the knowledge of God, and we are taking every thought captive to the obedience of Christ.

2 Corinthians 10:5

Reflection

One reason we get stuck in the same old sins is because our minds follow familiar patterns, and it's hard to create new ones. Then, as you do the same things over and over, Satan gets you to buy into the lie that your situation is hopeless. His goal is to get you to believe that by nature you are a drug addict or a manipulator or a negative person, that you are controlled by fear or shame, that nothing will ever change, and so on. Once you give in to and adopt this line of thinking, the entrenched fortresses become difficult to remove. Your behavior deteriorates even more because people always act according to who they believe they are.

The only solution is to tear down these fortresses by "taking every thought captive to the obedience of Christ" (2 Corinthians 10:5). Reprogram your mind and release yourself from captivity. This is how you unleash your full potential and free yourself up to then help other men rise to do the same.

The solution is twofold but straightforward. First, identify Christ's thoughts on a matter, and second, align your own thinking under the rule of His truth. The truth, then, will set you free (John 8:32).

Action

1. How has a sense of hopelessness impacted your life or decisions recently or in the past?
2. According to God's Word, is there ever a time to lack hope?
3. What area of your life needs a boost in hope?

Prayer

Jesus, give me hope. Renew my hope in Your saving power. Restore my hope in Your plan. Let me see things and experience things that will expand my hopefulness in a new way. In Your name, amen.

But I say, walk by the Spirit, and you will not carry out the desire of the flesh.

Galatians 5:16

Reflection

One of the most important lessons to learn in your development as a young man is that your own choices are what lead to a dire state of distress in your life. You must remove blaming others from your vocabulary. God allows the consequences to play out because He wants you to learn from your sins and to discover how to control your emotions.

I'm sure you've watched football or another sport where emotions can get out of hand. It could be during a playoff game, when everything is on the line. And then, because of heated emotions, one player shoves another, and the one who was shoved punches back. Because the first shove wasn't seen, the player who responded is the one who is penalized. Games have been lost this way. No matter what has happened to you, do not make the situation worse with your response. Keep your eye on the true goal at hand.

One of the goals God has in either allowing or creating a crisis point in your life is to force your return to Him. When your departure from Him leads to living out of alignment with His will, God will often permit difficulties to arise that can help get you back on track.

Action

1. Why is it important to accept responsibility for the difficulties you face in life?
2. What do blame and regret prevent, or possibly lead to, in a person's life?
3. What is one way to overcome feelings of blame and hurt from the past?

Prayer

Jesus, enable me to keep my eye on the overarching goal. Help me to see how hard I have worked to get here so that I do not lose it all through a wrong emotional response to difficulties in my life. In Your name, amen.

The LORD is the one who goes ahead of you; He will be with you. He will not fail you or forsake you. Do not fear or be dismayed.

Deuteronomy 31:8

Reflection

When it comes to God and His plans for your life, your physical lineage, standing, and position don't matter. All that matters is who goes with you. It's a simple spiritual point but one we often gloss over to our own detriment. The key to accomplishing any impossible task is the presence of the Lord with you. It doesn't depend on your expertise or lack thereof. It doesn't even depend on your strength. Your strategy is no match for God's, so you might as well table it and follow Him. Spiritual success in spiritual war depends entirely upon spiritual solutions. Spiritual solutions take place if, and when, God goes before you or with you. That determines your outcome.

God either needs to go before you or with you to overcome the enemy at hand. His presence is your power. His wisdom secures your win. And remember, it's always okay to ask for confirmation on something as important as that. Valiant warriors in God's kingdom know their own limits. Just as Gideon set out the fleece to be sure he was hearing from God correctly, you can ask God for your own signs of confirmation. As long as what you believe He is telling you does not contradict His Word, Scripture, you are free to move forward based on His confirming His path for you.

Action

1. Why is it important to let go of your own strategies in order to embrace God's?
2. What is one thing holding you back from doing that?
3. Describe the difference between spiritual solutions and physical solutions to life's challenges.

Prayer

Jesus, help me to pause and truly step back from trying to run my own show. I don't want to get in the way of what You are doing. Show me how to get a better idea of Your strategies for overcoming spiritual obstacles in my life. In Your name, amen.

Blessed are you when people insult you and persecute you, and falsely say all kinds of evil against you because of Me. Rejoice and be glad, for your reward in heaven is great; for in the same way they persecuted the prophets who were before you.

Matthew 5:11–12

Reflection

We don't normally associate a blessing with hardship and persecution. We don't naturally connect these things. When we dig deeper into the meaning of the Greek term translated here as persecuted, it makes it even more difficult to see the blessing connection. The literal translation means to be harassed. It refers to being treated in an evil, negative manner. This can include insults, abuse, vicious speech, and even false accusations.

Just writing those things down makes me wince. It probably does the same for you when you read them. None of us enjoys being bullied. None of us volunteers for harassment. But Jesus tells us we are blessed for being bullied for righteousness' sake. Keep in mind, He doesn't say you and I are blessed for being bullied for just any reason. The blessing is tied to the why behind it.

The people blessed are those persecuted or harassed for the sake of His name, His righteousness, or His kingdom agenda. This type of persecution comes about when you are choosing to do or say the right thing for righteous reasons, and you face fallout for your choice. When you are facing persecution because you are living out the values of the kingdom of God and you are associated with Jesus Christ, that is when you can expect a blessing.

Action

1. What does being persecuted for righteousness mean to you personally?
2. What is one way to overcome any hesitancy you may have in facing persecution?

Prayer

Jesus, enable me to see the big picture when things don't go well. Show me how to look for the blessing when I'm facing various trials related to living for Your kingdom. I want to praise You even in the midst of the difficult seasons of life. In Your name I pray, amen.

Remember the word that I said to you, "A slave is not greater than his master." If they persecuted Me, they will also persecute you; if they kept My word, they will keep yours also. But all these things they will do to you for My name's sake, because they do not know the One who sent Me.

John 15:20–21

Reflection

If you are not facing spiritual persecution or opposition of any kind, then you can pretty much assume that you are not living a godly life. If there are absolutely no negative repercussions coming upon you because of your faith and the choices you make based on it, then your faith is not being clearly demonstrated. You are a secret-agent Christian, or a spiritual CIA operative. Persecution is part and parcel of the process of kingdom living.

When you decided to live as a visible Christian because you wanted to align yourself with the values system of the kingdom of God, you decided to be a problem in our culture. The further a culture moves away from a Christian worldview, the more those who hold to and live according to kingdom values will appear to be peculiar and will be persecuted.

Now, to appear peculiar doesn't mean you are to be intentionally weird. It just means you will stand out as stepping to the beat of a different drummer. You will set yourself apart from the crowd as someone who listens to a different voice and adheres to a different standard called righteousness. As followers of Jesus, we demonstrate that peace is more productive than chaos. We demonstrate that love is more powerful than hate. We reveal that families can stay together, and that employees can work hard even when no one is around to see what they are doing. We raise the standard, and in doing so, we invite persecution. The same level of hate, vitriol, and persecution that Jesus experienced can potentially come at you as well.

But with spiritual persecution comes the promise of blessing. In order to reap this, we need to be open to the working of God in and through our lives through this kingdom value.

Action

1. Do you feel ready to face persecution for Christ? If not, why not?
2. How can you find strength in others as you face possible persecution?

Prayer

Jesus, I want to be willing to suffer as you suffered. Help me not to give in to the pressure around me, but to stand strong for you. I pray this in Your name, amen.

> For whoever has, to him more shall be given, and he will have an abundance; but whoever does not have, even what he has shall be taken away from him.
>
> Matthew 13:12

Reflection

God desires to raise you up to serve Him in a mighty conquest to advance His kingdom agenda. But prior to taking you there, He asks you to be obedient in what He has called you to do right now. Matthew 13:12 summarizes this principle of demonstrating faithfulness right where you are before God gives you more responsibility in His kingdom.

Faithfulness with what you have right now and right where you are is always the first step toward further use in God's kingdom. We see this in the life of Shamgar in Judges 3:31. God wants to know whether you are willing to follow Him right where you are. He wants to see what you are willing to do right now at school or at home—with your family and friends. Don't waste your time on visions of grandeur if you are not willing to begin by achieving the small victories that are yours to grab first.

Let God use you where you are. Let Him see your willingness to follow Him. As He does, He will make your next move clear to You. You don't need to figure out how to get to the dreams He has placed in your soul. You just need to be faithful with each step in front of you right now.

Action

1. What is one way you can be obedient right now with what God has given you to serve Him?
2. Have you witnessed God expand His use of you over time?
3. Why is it easy to get frustrated when dreams and visions do not quickly come to pass?

Prayer

Jesus, I don't want to waste my life swinging for the fences when You are asking me to get on first base first. Help me to be obedient where I am right now. I trust that You will take me down the path of greatest impact. In Your name, amen.

Have I not commanded you? Be strong and courageous! Do not tremble or be dismayed, for the Lᴏʀᴅ your God is with you wherever you go.

Joshua 1:9

Reflection

While God provides pockets of peace in moments of uncertainty, our humanity leaves us vulnerable to ongoing emotional changes based on what we've been tasked with. Obedience as a young man isn't always couched in calm. Sometimes that obedience takes place in a mixture of emotions. Courage does not mean the absence of fear. Courage means right actions taken in spite of fear's presence.

There's nothing courageous about doing something you know will succeed without any opposition. Courage is evidenced when you rise up to do the task that looks impossible.

It can be frustrating when circumstances don't appear to be in your favor. It is disappointing when you want to be the person you know you can be, but things haven't fallen into place. It can take a toll on anyone's patience when dreams rise up within, but life seems to be solely devoted to surviving each day. You know you were made for more. You know you can accomplish more. You feel stuck. But remember, even though waiting can be frustrating, when God decides to move, He can shift the landscape overnight. I've seen Him do it in my own life many times. I've also seen Him do it for others. When God is ready, it doesn't take long. He can turn a servant in a field into a Baal fighter leading the charge to freedom for a whole nation. He did it for Gideon, and He can do it for you.

Action

1. Describe the difference between spiritual courage based on God's definition and humanity's courage based on cultural norms.
2. Why does it take courage to follow God?
3. Do other people always get to witness someone's courageous acts? Why or why not?

Prayer

Jesus, give me greater courage to follow You. I want to be used by You to advance Your kingdom agenda on this earth. Help me to have the wisdom needed to do just that. In Your name, amen.

For the LORD your God is the one who goes with you, to fight for you against your enemies, to save you.

Deuteronomy 20:4

Reflection

Part of rising up as a young man involves doing what God says even when it doesn't make sense. As long as the way you think God is leading you doesn't contradict His revealed principles in His Word, and you have received confirmation from Him to get going, you are to go. Your response to His leading often plays a larger role in the outcome than the strategy itself. When God is ready to move, it doesn't matter how big your enemy is. It doesn't matter how entrenched the opposition is or how shattered your world is. Nothing and no one can override God when He sets His mind on victory.

We exist today in the midst of a pagan nation, on many levels. We are sorely outnumbered as disciples in the body of Christ. The secular world has not only abandoned God, but it has taken up the offensive against the one true God. It is oppressing the church and the truth of Scripture in many ways. This is our cultural reality, whether we like it or not. We can pretend it doesn't exist, but that won't change what we are facing.

It doesn't take millions to take back ground for Christ, though. It only takes a few committed men. We are to rise up and do what

God has called each of us to do so that we might advance His kingdom agenda on earth.

Action

1. Have you ever done what God told you to do when it didn't make sense? If so, what was the result?
2. In what ways does the culture oppress Christian values in our land?
3. What is the greatest thing you have ever accomplished for God's kingdom?

Prayer

Jesus, the need for us to rise up as kingdom men is great. I raise my voice in obedience to Your calling. I offer myself to You as a kingdom warrior to advance Your cause in our land and around the world. In Your name, amen.

For the LORD your God dried up the waters of the Jordan before you until you had crossed, just as the LORD your God had done to the Red Sea, which He dried up before us until we had crossed; that all the peoples of the earth may know that the hand of the LORD is mighty, so that you may fear the LORD your God forever.

Joshua 4:23–24

Reflection

When you read Joshua 4, you'll discover how setting up markers or memorials can help you not only in your personal faith but also in encouraging and helping others in their walk with God. We see in this chapter that the Lord had done a miraculous work in drying up the Jordan and allowing the people to cross it unhindered so that "all the peoples of the earth may know that the hand of the Lord is mighty, so that you may fear the Lord your God forever" (Joshua 4:24). The Lord commanded the Israelites to set up a marker at the site. The memorial was not only to remind themselves and the next generation of the event, producing a greater fear of God in their hearts, but it was also there to proclaim God's might to the world.

The Israelites were crossing into the Promised Land. But the Promised Land was full of evil. God wanted the Israelites to know that even though evil would surround them, He had them in His hand. God also wanted the Canaanites, Hittites, Amorites, and others to hear the stories about what He had done for the Israelites. He wanted them to hear of the miracles He had done in their midst. He chose to show off what He had done so their enemies would know His strength, so they would gain a better idea of what, and Whom, they were up against. God set out to establish the reputation of the Israelites as a nation whose God was over all.

We need to remember those times when God showed up and showed out, stepping into our situations to do something everyone thought was impossible. We are never to forget those times. We must also be intentional about making these miraculous moments known to others so they will fear God and honor Him too.

Action

1. Describe any reminders or markers that help you reflect on God's involvement in your life. If you don't have any, have you witnessed someone else's?

2. Why is it important to consider God's past actions as we approach our present realities?

3. What things cause us to quickly forget what God has done for us in the past and inhibit us from telling others?

Prayer

Jesus, I want to remember Your movement in my life on a more regular basis so that I can draw from those seasons a deeper level of faith and courage for what I face right now. Show me how to set up markers to help me remember Your faithful hand in all things. In Your name, amen.

And I will make you a great nation,
And I will bless you,
And make your name great;
And so you shall be a blessing;
And I will bless those who bless you,
And the one who curses you I will curse.
And in you all the families of the earth will be blessed.

Genesis 12:2–3

Reflection

As a young man who follows the Lord, you have the freedom and opportunity to bless those around you. The blessing is a way to spread and encourage God's gifts, protection, and rule in their lives. It's not about giving those you bless a goal or a future role to aim toward. Let them choose their own goals and roles based on their own thoughts and desires and the Lord's leading. Neither is it about giving them stuff, as we've looked at in earlier devotions. Rather, transferring the blessing is always about affirming God's favor and will for the lives of those who are being blessed.

Keep in mind, to be blessed in the Bible meant you were to also become a blessing to others. It's never only about you.

When you seek to pass on the blessing to someone else, or when you seek to receive a blessing from someone else, remember that it is not about helping someone make a name for themselves. Or for you, for that matter. It isn't even about identifying skills and talents to explore. Living in the kingdom blessing means learning to live in divine favor, which then spills out onto how others both perceive and treat you. It is about what God wants to do in you, for you, and through you.

Action

1. Of the three aspects of a blessing—God's gifts, protection, and rule—which is most important to you and why?
2. Why is it important to allow those you seek to bless the freedom to make their own decisions about their future?
3. Have you ever been held back by someone trying to dictate your choices under the guise of blessing? What was the result?

Prayer

Jesus, make me an instrument of Your divine benefit, divine protection, and divine dominion to those around me. I want to be a conduit of the blessing from God to others. Show me what I need to adjust in my own life to position myself to live this out more fully. In Your name, amen.

Whatever you do, do your work heartily, as for the Lord rather than for men, knowing that from the Lord you will receive the reward of the inheritance. It is the Lord Christ whom you serve.

Colossians 3:23–24

Reflection

You can measure the destiny of a team—whether that be a family, work group, business, church, community, or even nation—by its leadership. Unfortunately, today we face a crisis of leadership. People don't know who to follow anymore because this crisis has produced a number of poor models and mentors and a complete and utter lack of great leaders.

Yet, God's kingdom program is designed around this process of transferring spiritual wisdom, known as discipleship, in order to produce future leaders. One of your primary roles as a young man is to lead others in the way they should go. Another term we often use for leaders is *influencers*. The issue is never whether a man is a leader. As a man who follows God, you are a leader by nature of your calling. The issue is whether you will be a great leader or a poor one.

To be a poor leader requires little effort on your part. But to be a leader who truly influences those around you to rise up and pursue the advancement of God's kingdom agenda requires a level of courage that many lack today. It is countercultural to lead people in biblical values. Only men who understand and embrace this reality will be able to suffer the slings of the enemy with dignity and grace as they pursue the preparation of the next generation to serve Christ.

Action

1. How does a crisis of leadership show up at school?
2. How does a crisis of leadership show up in relationships?
3. How does a crisis of leadership show up in a cultural setting?

Prayer

Jesus, make me part of the solution and not part of the problem. I do not want to contribute to a crisis of leadership in any manner. Raise my internal standards of what it means to truly live as a kingdom man so that I fully live out and experience the leadership role I am called to fulfill. In Your name, amen.

This is My commandment, that you love one another, just as I have loved you. Greater love has no one than this, that one lay down his life for his friends. You are My friends if you do what I command you.

John 15:12–14

Reflection

To exercise your biblical manhood through a position of influence, you need to know where you are headed. You need to have a vision. Visions aren't often birthed in silos. Visions are formulated through studying the lessons of the past and the leaders of the present and combining that with your calling and the calling of those under your care.

A young man can do this by listening to those above him and around him. A great mind remains moldable and open to learning from others and following guidance with humility. A great leader constantly works on improving his skills and his game. One way to do this is by studying, listening, and asking questions of those in leadership roles. Godly leadership requires both following and leading through a mutual commitment expressed by both men in a relationship, or in the groups of men being poured into.

To live apart from relationships that allow you to encourage and edify each other is to fail to fulfill the mandate to make disciples and also to grow spiritually. Life on life is where growth takes place. This requires intentionality, humility, and most important, commitment.

Action

1. Where do you see yourself in five years from a spiritual and influential standpoint?
2. What steps do you need to take this week and this year to set yourself on a path to achieve the five-year vision you have for yourself?
3. In what ways can you listen more openly to godly men who have been placed in your life to influence you for good?

Prayer

Jesus, I hope that by listening to and learning the wisdom of those who have grown more than I have, I will continue to develop into a kingdom man who can impact and influence others. I want to develop more personal relationships with men that will allow us all to benefit and develop more fully. In Your name, amen.

Let us not lose heart in doing good, for in due time we will reap if we do not grow weary.

Galatians 6:9

Reflection

Achieving greatness in this life often comes as a result of many strengths merged together. Rarely does one man rise to accomplish tremendous things all on his own. There's typically a coach, parent, mentor, pastor, friend, neighbor, teammate, sibling, or teacher—or a combination of those and others—who helps create the context for success. As a young man, you need to recognize the value of and need for contributors in every aspect of the equation who are committed to a shared overarching goal.

Unfortunately, commitment has gone missing. We don't see a lot of commitment around. People quit very easily in our culture, especially when things get tough. They give up on school, jobs, or relationships the moment things get a little tough. As a young man who wishes to follow God, it is good to value commitment and live it out.

Action

1. Describe what happens when you stop seeing results from the investment of your time and energy in a project or person.
2. How does Galatians 6:9 speak into this situation?
3. How has our contemporary culture impacted individuals' ability to persevere with tenacity and diligence?

Prayer

Jesus, enable me to keep going even when I don't see any fruit for the effort I am putting forward. Remind me how important it is to keep the faith and trust the outcome to Your hands. Please also give me hints along the way to help me know that I am not alone in my desire to impact other people's lives. In Your name, amen.

But the greatest among you shall be your servant.

Matthew 23:11

Reflection

A fundamental rule of biblical manhood is that you don't get to the top without serving first. You don't wake up number one. What's more, a true man of God never stops serving.

Unfortunately, today we have a lot of men who want to skip serving and get to the top quickly. They want to skip the hard work, dedication, and tenacity required for greatness. I have had young pastors ask me numerous times over the years what the secret is for building a church the size and scope of ours. I know what they mean by the question because there really is no secret at all. They are looking for a secret, but none exists. Common sense tells you it took hard work, grit, commitment, and humility through serving when no one was watching, when the lights were out, and no one knew your name. Effort has become a lost quality in our land.

It takes hard work to unleash and achieve greatness, no matter if you're in school or in the workforce. And a good part of that hard work involves your willingness to serve. Jesus put it this way in Matthew 23:11: "But the greatest among you shall be your servant."

Action

1. What are some thoughts you entertain that keep you from seeking to serve others or to become more involved in your local body of believers?
2. What would happen to an athletic team who lost their willingness to put in the effort to stay physically fit during the off-season?
3. In what ways has the culture shifted people toward an increased desire for quick success and instant fame?

Prayer

Jesus, I am willing to be patient as You move me along the pathway of development and growth. I am willing to serve those around me. I understand that life isn't about me and my desires. It is about connecting with others who share similar values and goals so that together we can advance Your kingdom agenda on earth. In Your name, amen.

But He answered them, "My Father is working until now, and I Myself am working."

John 5:17

Reflection

We have far too many men today who want to lead but don't want to follow. They want to lead but refuse to serve. They want to skip straight to number one without any experience at being number two, three, or even ten. But great leaders, great coaches, great men know that you only transfer authority and responsibility to those who have demonstrated the ability to handle it.

You ascend to greatness by first descending into a role of service. No one has ever just woken up as the president of a company or a chairman of the board. Key leaders serve their way to the top by performing in a manner that demonstrates the willingness, understanding, character, and responsibility to pull off even greater things.

That is a truism of life. Joshua had the privilege of the mountaintop experience because he was willing to serve in the valley. What's more, he was wise enough to serve. As a young man, you need to realize that to get somewhere in life, you need to learn from those who have gotten somewhere in life. You need to listen. Observe. Take notes. Ask questions. Contribute. Study. Respect. Acknowledge. And serve.

Action

1. What are some practical ways you can start serving more?

2. Have you seen anyone ascend the ladder of success who carried within him or her a servant's heart? What did you learn from observing them?

3. How does our culture portray those who are willing to serve others, and does this positively or negatively impact people's desire to serve?

Prayer

Jesus, correct my thinking where I am wrong about the value of serving and investing in others. Give me biblical insight so I can see and understand how You view a servant's heart. Help me live my life for an audience of One, knowing that Your approval and favor is more meaningful than anything else I could ever have in my life. In Your name, amen.

Be strong and courageous, do not be afraid or tremble at them, for the LORD your God is the one who goes with you. He will not fail you or forsake you.

Deuteronomy 31:6

Reflection

A lot of young men are not growing spiritually today because they are not positioning themselves for growth. They are not placing themselves in the proximity of spiritual greatness. You can't run with carnal Christians and expect to rise as a kingdom man. You have to look for men who are already in the right spot. They may not be perfect, but they are close to God. In fact, that's one reason the disciples became such dynamic men. They knew where to hang out. They spent time with Christ. They knew to reject the spirit of fear in all things.

Any man who only sees how big the problem is does not have the right spiritual DNA. I sure don't need men around me telling me how big a problem is. Do you? If there's a giant, he's giant! You don't need to tell me he is a giant. Always remember who you are. In Christ, you are a giant-slayer, like David. You are a Baal fighter, like Gideon. Don't run when you face a giant. Instead, figure out how to maneuver around, climb over, barrel through, or simply out-strategize the opponent. Bottom line: Don't cower when giants tower over you.

Whatever you are facing today, even if it is looming large, casting shadows of doubt and producing feelings of fear, remember who you are in Christ. Remember the tools He has given you called faith, courage, and the rightful use of His name. You can overcome anything when you are connected to the One who rules over all. Let your hope rest in this truth.

Action

1. Describe what you are doing to position yourself for growth spiritually and as an influencer.

2. In what ways can you make yourself even more available to face and overcome obstacles?

3. What are some thoughts you have that encourage you to run away from or avoid conflict, especially spiritually based conflict, when there is a need for you to rise up and confront it?

Prayer

Jesus, increase my courage. Pour into me a greater level of faith that strengthens me when life's situations turn sour. Help me to stand up and act like a man of God to overcome whatever I'm facing. I ask for Your Spirit to be made manifest within me at a greater level than ever before. In Your name, amen.

I call heaven and earth to witness against you today, that I have set before you life and death, the blessing and the curse. So choose life in order that you may live, you and your descendants, by loving the LORD your God, by obeying His voice, and by holding fast to Him; for this is your life and the length of your days, that you may live in the land which the LORD swore to your fathers, to Abraham, Isaac, and Jacob, to give them.

Deuteronomy 30:19–20

Reflection

If you let them, adversity and challenges have a way of sharpening your skills, strengthening your will, and focusing your approach to your goals and dreams. They can cause you to rise higher than people ever expected you to go, or higher than you thought you would go. But it all depends on how you choose to view and respond to the difficulties that come your way. Will you respond in great faith, or will you respond in blame, bitterness, or fear? It's your choice. But whatever choice you make will also determine the outcome you—and generations after you—will face.

We are living in a day when the proverbial fork in the road is more pronounced than ever. When you examine all that is happening around us—the chaos, confusion, lack of clarity, and voices coming at us from all directions—it is clear that it is time for men to make a choice. Will you choose wisely and live? Or will you choose poorly? Cultural change starts with one man making one wise decision and then the next. And it starts right now, with you.

Action

1. Describe a time you chose death through your actions. What was the result?
2. In what ways can you choose life through your words, thoughts, and actions?
3. What would it take to see a true cultural impact of kingdom values in our land today?

Prayer

Jesus, focus my thoughts and my goals on everyday life so that I do not miss opportunities to choose life in all I think, say, and do. Encourage me through Your presence so I can see the impact wisdom has not only on my life but on the lives of those around me. In Your name, amen.

Be on the alert, stand firm in the faith, act like men, be strong.

1 Corinthians 16:13

Reflection

Young men who follow God should live a life that both models for others how to live according to spiritual principles of manhood and guides them in doing so. When David went up against Goliath, he faced awful odds, according to the world's standards. Everyone was calling on Goliath to win and to win easily. Many men would have cowered beneath an opponent the world predicted to win. But that's not what kingdom men do. Godly men don't cower. Godly men don't listen to the odds. Godly men rise to overcome the obstacles at hand. They certainly don't run from them.

As godly men, we are to rise above the obstacles looming large before us in our land. We must never back down or seek to avoid them. Instead, we are to set a new standard. Establish a new pace. Boldly declare that we, as men, no longer accept the evil nor the divisions that the culture demands remain. We must do this for ourselves, but we also must do this with and for each other. When you commit to living your life as a man of God, it isn't about being a lone-ranger Christian. You are choosing to identify with men who will collectively respond to the need for a fresh troop of kingdom warriors to take our stand.

Action

1. In what ways are you intentionally modeling how to live according to spiritual principles of manhood?
2. How can you use your relationships and activities to do this more?
3. Is there anything you need to improve in your life regarding your connection to other godly men or your willingness to disciple others?

Prayer

Jesus, help me to see how I can be more intentional about modeling what it looks like to live as a fully dedicated kingdom man. Show me where I need to be more willing to connect with other men to be discipled or to disciple others. In Your name, amen.

But the wisdom from above is first pure, then peaceable, gentle, reasonable, full of mercy and good fruits, unwavering, without hypocrisy.

James 3:17

Reflection

What you choose matters. Your decisions impact others. You can choose life by basing your decisions on the wisdom of God's Word. His commandments, precepts, and principles exist to show you how to live a life of wisdom.

As you make your choices throughout your days, there are a lot of conflicting and tempting options out there. They may seem right. They may look enticing. But the real question is whether your choice is one that Jesus would authorize and endorse. Because if it's not what Jesus would authorize or endorse, all you will experience is disintegration and ultimate death in whatever it is you are pursuing. Wrong choices lead to failure, frustration, and loss.

But if you choose wisely, the truth of God's Word will bring life, not only to you but also to those around you. By applying God's wisdom to your life and by living in accordance with what He has outlined in Scripture, you are setting yourself up for spiritual success. Wisdom is the way to experience God's will and His favor because wisdom is the application of God's will to the practical areas of life.

Action

1. Describe a time when one of your choices, or a culmination of choices, negatively impacted you or someone you love. What did you learn from that?

2. Describe a time when one of your choices, or a culmination of choices, positively impacted you or someone you love. What did you learn from that?

3. How can you better seek to know and apply God's truth in your life?

Prayer

Jesus, my choices impact my life and the lives of others for good or for bad. Help me to recognize this and take it to heart so that I will walk with wisdom and move forward with grace in all I think, say, and do. In Your name, amen.

The LORD arises to contend,
And stands to judge the people.
The LORD enters into judgment with the elders and
    princes of His people,
"It is you who have devoured the vineyard;
The plunder of the poor is in your houses."

Isaiah 3:13–14

Reflection

The choice to live as a man of God or not is yours to make. But while the choice is yours, I want to remind you that you don't get to choose the consequences. All consequences are in the hand of God. Isaiah 3 makes it clear what happens when men do not choose well.

As a result of abdicating their biblical kingdom roles, the men became weak and fell by the sword (Isaiah 3:25). Unfortunately, this all sounds very familiar. Too many men are operating outside of their divinely ordained responsibilities, thus causing all of us to fall by the sword of societal unrest. What we need are men who are willing not only to declare that they are kingdom men, as Joshua did in Joshua 24, but also to live like they are.

This declaration is to be made manifest in what you think, say, and do. It is to show up in how you carry yourself in culture, how you conduct your responsibilities, and how you interact with others. A young man's choices should have a ripple effect on all he comes near, to bring about the greater good for everyone and usher in a larger display of God's glory.

Action

1. What would you say is God's purpose for applying consequences to our choices?
2. In what way can negative consequences turn into a positive experience in a young man's life?
3. Describe a major lesson you learned from experiencing negative consequences.

Prayer

Jesus, help me never to waste the consequences You allow in my life, which are there to teach me and help me develop into a kingdom man. Give me wisdom to learn and humility to apply what I have learned so that I can grow as a man and serve You and Your purposes for my life more than I ever have before. In Your name, amen.

If it is disagreeable in your sight to serve the LORD, choose for yourselves today whom you will serve: whether the gods which your fathers served which were beyond the River, or the gods of the Amorites in whose land you are living; but as for me and my house, we will serve the LORD.

Joshua 24:15

Reflection

One thing a young man should never forget is that God has an exclusivity clause. He cannot be second. My great concern with all of the cultural turmoil we are going through is that while many men may be calling on God and praying to God, they also have idols competing for and consuming their attention. These so-called American idols are sophisticated. Subtle. An idol might be technology. It could be politics. Celebrities. Sports. Status. It might even be one's race, entertainment, or what school they got into. As I've stated before, anything that overrules God in your decision-making—including another relationship—is an idol.

When you exalt an idol over God, you have removed Him from the equation. This is because God will excuse Himself from participating or intervening, even though you may be praying to Him for help.

It is only when young men stand up, stand strong, and declare what is right and true that God will bless them and use them for his kingdom. Joshua's declaration in Joshua 24 did not deny the reality of the day nor the humanity of each man, but it did state that these things were to be subject to a higher authority and greater good. To sum it up, he declared that he would put God first.

Action

1. What are some idols that take your attention away from God?
2. How have these idols brought you benefit over the course of your life or in any of your relationships?
3. Why is it important to turn from idols and turn toward the living God in all you think, say, and do?

Prayer

Jesus, reveal to me the areas where I still need to address any hidden idolatry I have in my life. Help me to turn from idolatry and turn toward You in my thoughts and actions. Enable me to disciple other men to recognize idols in their own lives as well. In Your name, amen.

Therefore be careful how you walk, not as unwise men but as wise, making the most of your time, because the days are evil. So then do not be foolish, but understand what the will of the Lord is.

Ephesians 5:15–17

Reflection

Far too many young men want a cafeteria god. This is the kind of god that you can pick and choose with, deciding when you want him and when you don't. That's not the kind of God that God is, and that's not the kind of man He is looking to partner with in impacting the world. God doesn't want you aligning with Him just in private. He is not seeking a silent majority. God calls each of us to publicly declare our allegiance to Him above all else. It is then that He will join us to address the issues at hand.

God has something to say on every subject and issue that confronts us, and He has not stuttered. Yes, the past may house its mistakes. But we can start right now to make a better tomorrow. We can start when each young man personally declares he will serve God in all he thinks, says, and does. That is not to say you will do this perfectly, but if your intention is to make God your priority, He will honor your heart.

Action

1. Why is it important to let go of your past and not allow the negativity in it to influence your present and future?
2. In what ways do you place God in the highest position in your life?
3. Have you seen a ripple effect from your actions that had a positive impact on others? What did you learn from it?

Prayer

Jesus, give me the grace I need to let go of the past and focus on the present. Help me to recognize Your presence in my present situations so that I can honor You with my actions. Show me the way to go and the path I need to take to live out the destiny You have created me for. In Your name, amen.

Then David said to his son Solomon, "Be strong and courageous, and act; do not fear nor be dismayed, for the Lord God, my God, is with you. He will not fail you nor forsake you until all the work for the service of the house of the Lord is finished."

1 Chronicles 28:20

Reflection

David was a young man who didn't cower in front of a giant. That's one reason God chose him to eventually become king. Saul and the armies of Israel looked at Goliath and trembled. David saw the giant and strategized a plan for his defeat. David didn't let his fear overtake him. In fact, David put his fear in its rightful place.

Likewise, godly men are not to run away in the face of adversity. Godly men are not to bail out when the going gets tough. You know as well as I do that it is cowards who run in the face of challenge. It is cowards who bail. But true, authentic, and strong men of God rise up, because when everyone else is chanting, "We can't," there's one voice that quietly yet firmly responds, "Why not?" With God, you can do anything.

If a shepherd boy can slay a giant with a stone, there is no telling what God can do through you and through me. God has given you the tools you need to overcome whatever obstacles you face and to march forward on a mission to expand His glory and advance His kingdom agenda.

Action

1. What is your natural inclination when you face conflict or a difficult challenge that could cost you something?

2. What are some reminders you can position in your life to help you regain confidence and faith in God when difficulties come?

3. Where do you think David drew his courage from, especially since he was so young? What can you learn from him?

Prayer

Jesus, increase my level of faith and my confidence in You so I can live more courageously as a godly young man. I do not want to shrink back when adversity comes my way. I want to be the strong leader my loved ones need me to be for them. In Your name, amen.

> Now Jabez called on the God of Israel, saying, "Oh that You would bless me indeed and enlarge my border, and that Your hand might be with me, and that You would keep me from harm that it may not pain me!" And God granted him what he requested.
>
> 1 Chronicles 4:10

Reflection

It's hard to transfer, or give to someone else, something that was never given to you. Many men never received the blessing from another man of God. You may never have had a man guide you toward kingdom values in your personal development. But even if your life has been filled with challenges, difficulties, and spiritual gaps, you can still gain access to the blessing. Divine favor, dominion, and authority are rightfully yours as a child of the King. All you need to do is ask Him for it.

Perhaps you have no lineage worth revisiting. You have no heritage passed down that is worth honoring. Maybe your mom or your dad resented you as it seems that Jabez's mom resented carrying him, naming him "pain" (1Chronicles 4:9). Maybe when you hear other people speaking about families, your heart doesn't fill up with fond memories, but only feels an ache.

But Jabez didn't let his family define him. Your past doesn't define you either. Jabez didn't let what other people felt about him or said about him become his identity. Like any man of God, Jabez desired more. He desired the blessing. So he went directly to the

Source. What's more, he got it. And you can too. Go to God. God has a great blessing in store for you.

Action

1. In what ways did you receive a transfer of the biblical blessing, and in what ways do you feel you did not receive it?
2. How can you be sure you are spending your life to pass on the blessing to those under your care?
3. In what ways have others let you know that you have passed the blessing down to them, and how did that make you feel?

Prayer

Jesus, make me aware of every situation where I can pass the blessing on to someone under my care. Please bring about situations that will give me greater courage and motivation to provide others with a spiritual blessing. Help me to lead through loving You and to learn from those who also love You. In Your name, amen.

Bear one another's burdens, and thereby fulfill the law of Christ.

Galatians 6:2

Reflection

Awakening our biblical manhood requires the commitment and the discipline to honor God in all we do. But what we often forget is that this determination is frequently formed in us over the course of our lives. It doesn't just appear out of nowhere. We are in this together with other men of God. Nothing difficult we overcome ever rests solely on our own shoulders. That's one reason God emphasizes unity and the power of fellowship and discipleship throughout Scripture.

If you saw THE LORD OF THE RINGS film series, you likely remember one of the most famous scenes. It comes toward the end of *The Return of the King*. The main character, Frodo, whose role is to carry the burden of the evil ring to its destruction and thus save the world, has lost all strength. He is lying, unable to move forward. If he didn't make it to the top of the mountain to throw the ring in the fire, the quest would be lost.

That's when his companion, Sam, makes a bold move. Scooping Frodo up in his arms and lifting him onto his back, he carries Frodo when he can no longer move forward on his own. "Come on, Mr. Frodo," Sam says with all the strength he can muster. "I can't carry it for you, but I can carry you."[1] Similarly, sometimes we need others to carry us. And we can also do our part to lift, encourage, support, and draw near to those in need to help them finish the task of overcoming any evil that seeks to defeat them.

Action

1. Identify hesitancies you have toward asking others to help you carry your burdens.
2. In what ways can you overcome these hesitancies and fulfill your role as a young man?
3. What are some hindrances that keep you from helping others?

Prayer

Jesus, I want to be a greater help to other men in need. Show me how I can strengthen my own walk with You to be better positioned to help someone else. Give me wisdom about how I can use the gifts and grace You have given to me to support, encourage, and lift up men around me. In Your name, amen.

Notes

Day 44

1. Jared Staver, "Car Damage at Different Speeds," *Staver Legal Blog*, accessed July 29, 2024, https://www.chicagolawyer.com/speed-affect-car-accident-dama ges/.

Day 45

1. Casey Schwartz, "The Age of Distracti-pression," *New York Times*, July 9, 2022, https://www.nytimes.com/2022/07/09/style/medication-depression-anxi ety-adhd.html.

Day 90

1. *The Lord of the Rings: The Return of the King*, directed by Peter Jackson (Burbank, CA: New Line Cinema, 2003), DVD.

Dr. Tony Evans is the founder and senior pastor of Oak Cliff Bible Fellowship in Dallas, founder and president of The Urban Alternative, former chaplain of the Dallas Mavericks and the Dallas Cowboys, and author of over 125 books, booklets, and Bible studies. The first African American to earn a doctorate of theology from Dallas Theological Seminary, he has been named one of the 12 Most Effective Preachers in the English-Speaking World by Baylor University.

Dr. Evans also holds the honor of writing and publishing the first full-Bible commentary and study Bible by an African American.

His radio program, *The Alternative with Dr. Tony Evans*, broadcasts to millions of active listeners across hundreds of radio stations and digital outlets across the nation and around the world.

Dr. Evans launched the Tony Evans Training Center in 2017, an online learning platform providing quality seminary-style courses for a fraction of the cost to any person in any place. The TETC currently has over fifty courses to choose from and has a student population of over 2,000.

Dr. Tony Evans was married to Lois, his wife and ministry partner of over fifty years, until Lois transitioned to glory in late 2019. They are the proud parents of four, grandparents of thirteen, and great-grandparents of five. In November 2023, Dr. Tony and Carla Evans were married.

For more information, visit TonyEvans.org.